"Mary Hulst writes with great authority and verve. Her writing is balanced and mature but also fresh. I can't imagine a preacher who would not be blessed by her work."
Cornelius Plantinga Jr., author of *Reading for Preaching*

"Three words came to mind as I read this book: *honest, practical* and *personal. Honest* because this little gem of a book reminds those of us who have been preaching a while as well as those new to preaching that we can improve our preaching. Many of us will find ourselves in the stories she shares about preaching gone wrong. *Practical* because Mary doesn't just tell us that we could be doing better, she shares with us how we can improve. She guides us through small steps that will yield big dividends. And *personal* because, as someone who knows Mary, preaching matters to her and she is good at it. I can hear her voice as I read through the pages. The words on these pages are from a person who cares deeply about the Word and who cares about those who proclaim it. This is book is a must-have for anyone who proclaims the gospel."
Michelle R. Loyd-Paige, Calvin College, president of Preach Sista!

"Mary Hulst has the rare gift of not only being an extremely effective preacher, but also an extremely effective teacher of preaching. One particular virtue of this book is the way that it integrates excellence in biblical exegesis, theological interpretation, pastoral discernment, communication skills and interpersonal intelligence into one seamless vision. As a result, the book helps us envision how the highest ideals for ministry can be practiced in a realistic and sustainable way of life. This book promises to inspire both rookie and veteran preachers for seasons of vital and faithful ministry."
John D. Witvliet, Calvin Institute of Christian Worship, Calvin College and Calvin Theological Seminary

"There are multitudes of thick, heavy books on the theology and philosophy of preaching. There are multitudes of preachers trying to get into their pulpit with a sermon every week. In this book, Mary Hulst has distilled theology and philosophy into a field guide for active-duty preachers. Relatively new preachers will find courage and thoughtful answers to the questions no one bothered to ask or answer in seminary (where do I hook my mic pack if I'm wearing a dress?). Seasoned preachers will find a fresh take on their work and encouragement to try something new or to return to their first love—telling the old, old story again and again."
Meg Jenista, pastor, Washington, DC Christian Reformed Church

"*A Little Handbook for Preachers* is an outstanding resource for those called to preach the gospel today. Much like the author and her sermons, the book is clear, insightful and inspired. Mary S. Hulst provides the essential principles for biblical preaching and offers practical and poignant advice on how to prepare a sermon that connects with the changing landscape of listeners in our churches today."
Josiah Chung, pastor, Living Water CRC, Grand Rapids, MI

"A wholly approachable and practical guide for those who take the call to preach seriously. Mary does not leave us full of shame for not preparing 'her way' but instead offers us a wealth of information, examples, stories and suggestions to encourage us to dig for the ways God will meet us as we go about the task of preaching. With each chapter, Mary reminds us of our own capacity for creativity and the possibility for connection—with God and those who will be moved by our words."
Austin Channing Brown, writer and speaker

"Mary Hulst presents an elegant and compelling vision of preaching as a vehicle of the gospel. For students taking this vehicle for their first test drive she offers an owner's manual; for experienced proclaimers who want to maximize their vehicles' performance she offers an important checklist. Her guiding principles help ensure that preaching excels in doing what God designs it to do—to nurture faithful, transformed lives."
Paul Scott Wilson, professor of homiletics, Emmanuel College, University of Toronto

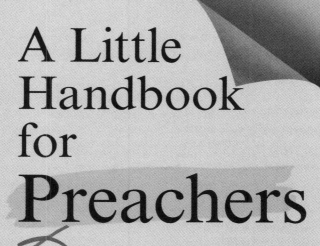

A Little Handbook for Preachers

Ten practical ways to a better sermon by Sunday

Mary S. Hulst

Foreword by Mark Labberton

IVP Books

An imprint of InterVarsity Press
Downers Grove, Illinois

InterVarsity Press
P.O. Box 1400, Downers Grove, IL 60515-1426
ivpress.com
email@ivpress.com

InterVarsity Press® is the book-publishing division of InterVarsity Christian Fellowship/USA®, a movement of students and faculty active on campus at hundreds of universities, colleges and schools of nursing in the United States of America, and a member movement of the International Fellowship of Evangelical Students. For information about local and regional activities, visit intervarsity.org.

Cover design: Cindy Kiple
Interior design: Beth McGill

Images: spiral notebook: Tharakorn/iStockphoto
        page curl: robynmac/iStockphoto
        highlighter elements: keeweeboy/iStockphoto

ISBN 978-0-8308-4128-8 (print)
ISBN 978-0-8308-9943-2 (digital)

Printed in the United States of America ♾

 As a member of the Green Press Initiative, InterVarsity Press is committed to protecting the environment and to the responsible use of natural resources. To learn more, visit greenpressinitiative.org.

Library of Congress Cataloging-in-Publication Data

Names: Hulst, Mary S., 1969- author.
Title: A little handbook for preachers : ten practical ways to a better
  sermon by Sunday / Mary S. Hulst.
Description: Downers Grove : InterVarsity Press, 2016. | Includes
  bibliographical references.
Identifiers: LCCN 2015050900 (print) | LCCN 2016000201 (ebook) | ISBN
  9780830841288 (pbk. : alk. paper) | ISBN 9780830899432 (eBook)
Subjects: LCSH: Preaching—Handbooks, manuals, etc.
Classification: LCC BV4211.3 .H855 2016 (print) | LCC BV4211.3 (ebook) | DDC
  251—dc23
LC record available at http://lccn.loc.gov/2015050900

| P | 20 | 19 | 18 | 17 | 16 | 15 | 14 | 13 | 12 | 11 | 10 | 9 | 8 | 7 | 6 | 5 | 4 | 3 | 2 | 1 |
| Y | 33 | 32 | 31 | 30 | 29 | 28 | 27 | 26 | 25 | 24 | 23 | 22 | 21 | 20 | 19 | 18 | 17 | 16 |

Lord, use this book to help your church.

Soli deo gloria.

Contents

Foreword

Mark Labberton

Praxis that's worth its salt is not just a Latin word for practice. Instead, it is a pointer to the convergence of theory and practice. Praxis holds ideas about something alongside and intertwined with our enactment of those ideas. The interaction, the corrective, the learning, the development of this dynamic relationship is our praxis.

Mary Hulst gives us here a book on the praxis of preaching. She artfully and pragmatically portrays theological and practical dimensions to preaching, surrendering neither and strengthening both. At times, Hulst is soaring in her vision of the nature of God who has spoken in Jesus Christ for the salvation of the world. This lands, however, as it does, in the solid reality (and mystery) of God's Word made flesh. Jesus Christ is the incarnation—the praxis—of God's saving love.

All faithful preaching both points to the Word made flesh and makes that Word flesh to its hearers. Therein lies the dual challenge for good preaching praxis. Hulst takes one of the most daunting and urgent aspects of pastoral ministry and lays it out before us with the care and thoroughness of a wise practitioner. She wants to help nurture preaching praxis that is grounded in

Scripture and in life, in theology and in discipleship, in concept and in expression, in framework and in delivery, in personal spiritual life and in communal life, in communication theory and in sermon delivery.

Though I am typically not one drawn to lists of "8 of this" or "5 of that" and "3 of the other," Hulst charms me by providing the kind of praxis help that I have sometimes needed and that I know others need too. She is not a "mere" sermonizer: she is a preacher who reflects on theology and the world, and a theologian who believes ordinary lives matter. No overdrawn hierarchies or exaggerated delineations between the elements. This feels like wisdom.

In the end, what I appreciate the most is that for Hulst praxis is not just the work of the preacher but eventually the work of every disciple. Strong preaching can be the catalyst for the process of God's Word being made flesh in the lives of God's people. When preaching does this work, it reflects the glory—the reality—of the One who has spoken about God and incarnated the life of God. This is the good news that the church and the world long to hear and see. This is the good news that best enables those who hear it to live it, making the praxis of faith what it is meant to be.

Introduction

If you're new to preaching, overwhelmed and intimidated, this book is for you.

If you've been preaching for a while and you're burned out and weary, this book is for you.

If you're looking for fresh ways to think about sermon preparation, this book is for you.

If you'd like some practical ways to enjoy preaching a little more, this book is for you.

If you're longing to have great conversations with your board, elders or congregation about preaching, this book is for you.

If you've gone to seminary or Bible college, this book will revive some of what you learned and hopefully will apply those lessons in helpful ways.

If you've not gone to seminary or Bible college, this book will give you a great place to start and point out other good books and resources that will help you.

If you're not a preacher, this book will be a behind-the-scenes tour of what goes into every sermon and will help you to listen better and help your preacher.

There's a Sunday every week. And for those of us who preach every week, those Sundays come all too soon. Some weeks the sermon falls into place beautifully, our delivery is sparkling, the congregation is attentive and we remember why we love this work. Other weeks—many weeks—we labor over commentaries, sketch out ideas, play with words, pray and practice and pray some more, and then we preach and it goes okay.

And for those of us who preach occasionally, it can be even harder to find a rhythm. Our sermon preparation time is stuck between our "day job" and the rest of life. Dwelling on a text, trying out ideas and practicing the sermon a time or two are luxuries. We long to preach well on a limited time budget.

Many of us know the creative mess that is preaching. We feel the frustration when things don't go the way we want and the delight when they do. There is much about preaching that is mysterious. And there is much about it that is incredibly practical. This book focuses on the latter.

This book is a practical guide to improving our preaching. Among other things, we'll talk about how to engage the Bible, how to focus on God, how to preach grace, how to deliver messages well and how to talk with your listeners about your preaching. Each chapter will give advice and suggestions to try.

You may want to read one chapter, work on that idea for a while and then move on to another chapter. You may want to skip ahead to a chapter you are most interested in. You may want to read through this book with a colleague or a small group. This book is a tool to help us preach better. How you use and apply the information here is up to you!

However you choose to engage this book, it's my hope that it encourages you in the act of preaching. Whether you preach sermons or listen to them, whether you teach people how to preach or have never been in a preaching class, my prayer is that this book will help you love preaching, love the Word, love the listeners and most of all love God even more.

As you read, note that all stories are fictional, though many are based on conversations I've had. For stories out of my own teaching, all identifying details have been changed to protect the identity of the students. Some of the material in chapter ten, "Getting Feedback About Your Preaching," first appeared in *The Banner* ("Preachers Are Like Peaches," December 23, 2012) and in *The Calvin Theological Seminary Forum* ("Not at the Door: Thoughts on When and Where to Talk About Sermons," Winter 2008).

When it comes to preaching, I too am trying my best. I would love to say that I hit the mark every week, and that I easily do everything I suggest in these pages. I don't. I try. I pray and read and write and practice, and then I preach. What keeps me at it, week after week, is what keeps all of us at it: we believe that God Almighty, Lord of heaven and earth, actually uses people like us to proclaim the mysteries of faith, and we are thrilled and humbled at this calling. So we try things and experiment and work hard, because there is nothing we would rather spend our lives getting right. I'm honored to be your companion in this work.

one

Biblical Preaching

FALLING IN LOVE WITH THE WORD

Most of us long to preach because there was something about the gospel story that grabbed us. For some of us it was because the gospel was our foundation in an otherwise unstable childhood. We may remember the flannel graphs and filmstrips that taught us about a God who cared deeply for his people— who cared deeply for us. For others the good news about Jesus echoed in the life of a parent or grandparent who shared his or her testimony with us again and again, shaping our own lives. Still others, like Paul, had our own Damascus Road moment, and we preach the good news because God gave us our lives back. Some of us left other careers—careers in which we made more money, had more prestige or were looking at a more secure retirement—in order to preach.

We love the gospel story. We love this story of a God who runs after his people and never lets them go. We love the stories that are easier to preach—anything out of Luke 15, the Daniel story of the three men in the fiery furnace, Jesus inviting the children to come—and we willingly wrestle with the passages that seem opaque, confusing or even dangerous, as when Jesus rejects his family or curses the fig tree, or most of the book of Judges.

Some of us have immersed ourselves in years of study, learned Greek vocabulary, sorted through Hebrew verbs and collected shelves of commentaries so that we can faithfully interpret this amazing story and apply it to the lives of those who listen. Some of us do our learning and preaching in addition to other jobs, pouring ourselves into this task because we want to spend our lives for the gospel.

We want to preach sermons that proclaim the good news that God loves sinners and has made a way for us to come home. We want to preach sermons that bring in the lost and disciple the found. We want to preach sermons that set people on fire. We want to raise the dead!

And then we get into a board meeting or meet with our worship committee and find that people want how-to sermons, sermons on the issue of the day or sermons that make their kids pay attention, and slowly, slowly, the gospel itself can fade right out of our preaching. We find ourselves giving advice, re-searching politics or coming up with gimmicks, and the love that drew us into the pulpit becomes faded and lifeless.

William Willimon, a Methodist bishop and professor at Duke Divinity School, describes that kind of postpreaching experience like this:

> The congregational consensus seemed to be that I preached it well enough. I received an unusual number of compli-ments at the end of the service (six, to be exact). They noted how engaging my sermon was, how helpful I was in explaining to their satisfaction what had long been for them a difficult Bible passage. More than one person ap-preciated my humor.
>
> From the serene vantage point of Monday, however, I now consider that sermon to be a moral failure. The reasons for this reassessment would require an explication

of the peculiar ethical demands for faithful Christian preaching. I am called to preach Christ and him crucified, not to make his gospel more accessible than he himself managed to make it.[1]

We want to preach Christ and him crucified. We want to be lovers of Scripture, animated by the Story that absorbs and illuminates our own stories.

So how do we keep that love alive? In the weekly grind of preaching, how do we shape our lives so that we love the Word?

> **We want to preach Christ and him crucified. We want to be lovers of Scripture, animated by the Story that absorbs and illuminates our own stories.**

Eugene Peterson loves Scripture. He began to translate it out of his love for it, and that paraphrase was published as *The Message*—of which over three million copies have been sold. Peterson says, "The challenge—never negligible—regarding the Christian Scriptures is getting them read, but read on their own terms, as God's revelation."[2] Spending time with someone like Peterson who deeply loves the Word reminds us of the power of the Story, and how much we want our story to be engulfed by that Story.

Christians, says Peterson, must not merely read the Bible in an effort to quarry out inspirational quotes to get them through their days. He warns, "It is possible to read the Bible from a number of different angles and for various purposes without dealing with God as God has revealed himself, without setting ourselves under the authority of the Father, the Son, and the Holy Spirit who is alive and present in everything we are and do." Instead, we need to "read the Bible the way it comes to us, not in the way we come to it."[3]

For Christians, and for Christian preachers in particular, loving the Word means allowing ourselves to be pulled into the revelation, to have our flaws revealed and our assumptions challenged, to have our ideas about God shattered when confronted by the truth that is God. We let ourselves be vulnerable before the Word, allowing the Spirit to weave it deep into us, convicting us of sin and calling us to holy living.

We cannot love something we hold at a distance, and that is never more true than when speaking about Christians' engagement with the Bible. Because it is a tangible object, something we can tuck in a bag and carry around, we forget that this is one of the primary ways that God speaks—Today! Right now!—to his people.

The work of the Holy Spirit animates our love of Scripture. He delights in showing us new facets of the jewel, shining the light of his love through the Word and allowing us the joy of seeing old words in a new way. Barbara Brown Taylor writes beautifully about this:

> For all the human handiwork that it displays, the Bible remains a peculiarly holy book. I cannot think of any text that has such authority over me, interpreting me faster than I can interpret it. It speaks to me not with the stuffy voice of some mummified sage but with the fresh, lively tones of someone who knows what happened to me an hour ago. Familiar passages accumulate meaning as I return to them again and again. They seem to grow during my absences from them; I am always finding something new in them I never found before, something designed to meet me where I am at this particular moment in time. This is, I believe, why we call the Bible God's "living" word.[4]

Loving the Word Means Taking the Time

Loving the Word means setting aside time each week for full engagement with the text. Of course, the amount of time needed to write a sermon varies with each preacher. Newer preachers may need more than twenty hours to research and write a sermon. Veteran preachers may be able to write a strong sermon in eight hours, and then take an hour or two for editing and oral practice. One researcher found that the average amount of time spent preparing a sermon was nine hours, but the range was from two to forty-one hours.[5]

Some of you would love to have twenty hours to prepare a sermon. But you're bivocational and trying to pastor a church while holding down a job. Others are full-time pastors, but the daily demands of running a church leave you scrambling for sermon preparation time. Ministry is a job where the urgent often swallows the important, meaning that preparing for preaching can so easily be short-changed.

In his book *Under the Unpredictable Plant*, Eugene Peterson tells the story of when he was so swamped by the demands of planting a church that he went to his Session (his leadership board) and resigned. He told them that was he was doing was not what he wanted to do. They asked him what he wanted to do, and he answered:

> "I want to study God's Word long and carefully so that when I stand before you and preach and teach I will be accurate. I want to pray, slowly and lovingly, so that my relation with God will be inward and honest. And I want to be with you, often and leisurely, so that we can recognize each other as close companions on the way of the cross and be available for counsel and encouragement to each other." . . .

One elder said, with some astonishment, "If that is what you want to do, why don't you do it? Nobody told you you couldn't, did they?" And I, with a touch of anger, said, "Because I have to run this church. Do you realize that running this church is a full-time job? There is simply no time to be a pastor."

Another elder said, "Why don't you let us run the church?" I said, "You don't know how." He said, "It sounds to me like you don't know how to be a pastor either. How about you let us learn how to run the church and we let you learn how to be a pastor?"[6]

So here is what we need to remember: despite what we think, other people can lead meetings. Other people can plan worship. Other people can teach Sunday school. Other people can even visit people in the nursing home. But *we* have been asked to preach. *We* have been entrusted to open God's Word and proclaim it to the people, and, as Peterson writes, that takes long and careful study.

Block Out the Time

The key is that each of us needs to allot time in our own schedules for however long it takes *us* to prepare well for preaching. Some of us can do great work in four hours. Others need twelve. As with many things, finding a good rhythm and sticking to it matters more than the details of that rhythm. Maybe you start early in the week, with Tuesday morning from 8 to noon set aside to begin the process (with no interruptions), and then you wrap up the writing on Friday afternoon, with a practice session early Sunday morning. Some people work better starting Friday and building to Sunday. When you have time blocked out for sermon preparation, it allows you to schedule the rest of your week around that time. Letting your elders, board or congregation know when you are writing your sermons also allows them to guard that time in your calendar and invites them to pray specifically for that part of your ministry on the day you are writing.

In a job where running the church can so quickly get in the way being a pastor, having blocks of time set aside for sermon preparation allows us to maintain our own investment in preaching. Of course there are emergencies, funerals and weddings that may squeeze our sermon preparation time. Every preacher knows that some sermons don't get the time they deserve. But we (and our elders or board!) need to value the preaching task enough to protect it.

Setting aside time for sermon preparation is a concrete way to demonstrate and practice our love of the Word. Instead of skimming through a passage for a quick hit, we have the time necessary to engage the text, read commentaries, think about the role of the passage in the life of the congregation and look for the leading of the Spirit. If we choose, we can spend time writing a thoughtful and articulate manuscript and then internalize that manuscript for delivery. Having a sermon manuscript or detailed outline completed well before the preaching event also allows us to work on the delivery of the sermon: reading it aloud, playing with gestures and movement, or shortening sentences so they are easy to deliver. Because we have spent time loving the Word and preparing our message, we know the sermon well enough to deliver it with confidence and are actually eager to preach. Our love for the Word becomes evident in the delight we take in preaching it.

When we are intentional in our sermon preparation, we not only display our love of the Bible but also reveal our love for our congregation. We love our people by loving the task of preaching. When asked which component of the church service has the most

When asked which component of the church service has the most impact on one's spiritual life, 35 percent of laypeople said the sermon, more than Communion (20 percent) or prayer (18 percent). Our investment in sermon preparation is an investment in the life of the church.

impact on one's spiritual life, 35 percent of laypeople said the sermon, more than Communion (20 percent) or prayer (18 percent).[7] Our investment in sermon preparation is an investment in the life of the church. As one layperson and communications scholar said to a group of preachers, "When you don't take the time to prepare a strong sermon, we all suffer."[8]

Dwell in the Word

One of the temptations of our preparation time is to spend hours looking at commentaries and word studies, and neglect dwelling on the passage itself. But as preaching professor turned seminary president Tim Brown says, "You can't get into the text unless the text first gets into you."[9] For Brown, this belief has led to the practice of memorizing every passage he preaches, and encouraging his students to do the same. Memorizing a passage lets us learn its cadence and rhythms and invites the text into our minds, hearts and lives in intimate ways.

To ensure that the Word has a primary spot in their thoughts for the week, other preachers print a copy of the week's passage and tape it to the bathroom mirror, allowing them to read and reread the text as they brush their teeth or shave. In *The Bible Study Handbook* Lindsey Olesburg suggests something she calls "manuscripting" the text: print it out in an easy-to-read font with a good amount of white space around the words and then circle words you don't understand, highlight strong words, write questions in the margins, draw lines connecting words with other words—engage the text.

Other preachers find it helpful to listen to the passage while driving or exercising (smartphone apps make this easy). Some even record themselves reading the passage and listen to that over the course of the week. One pastor I know writes his preaching text on a series of note cards and while he is on the treadmill or out walking the neighborhood he flips through the cards. All of these habits can feed our love of Scripture, and none of them takes an excessive amount of time.

Another practice to consider is *lectio divina* or "holy reading." While often used in corporate settings, *lectio divina* also provides a strong foundation for individual meditation on Scripture. In *lectio divina*, a short passage of Scripture is read aloud four times, with a period of silence between each reading. The first reading invites us to settle down and turn our thoughts toward the passage. After the second reading we choose a phrase from the passage to repeat in our minds, chewing on the words. Following the third reading we are invited to speak aloud a word or phrase from the passage. After the fourth reading we pray, using the words of the passage to guide our words to God. When practiced with a group, a sung refrain can be added between the readings that prepares us to hear the passage again. A good resource for learning more about this practice is *Discovering Lectio Divina: Bringing Scripture into Ordinary Life* by James C. Wilhoit and Evan B. Howard.

Other preachers find it helpful to pray through a passage by placing their name, the names of people they know or the name of their church in the passage. For example: "You, [Ryan, Dad, First Church], are the light of the world! A city built on a hill cannot be hid. No one after lighting a lamp puts it under the bushel basket, but on the lamp stand, and it gives light to all in the house. In the same way, [Ryan, Dad, First Church], let your light shine before others, so that they may see your good works and give glory to your Father in heaven." This practice reminds those of us who preach that the Word is alive for us and in us.

Whether we memorize the passage, meditate on it or pray through it, these patient disciplines move us away from thinking about the passage to dwelling in the passage. We can practice these disciplines as we drive, exercise or wait in line. As much as we love to learn *about* the Word, practices like these help us to love the Word itself.

IDEAS FOR DWELLING IN THE WORD

- Memorize the passage.
- Print out a copy and hang it where you'll see it.
- "Manuscript" the text.
- Listen to the passage.
- Put it on note cards.
- Practice *lectio divina*.

Learn All About It

When journalists go to interview a source, they prepare a list of questions to ask. In the same way, we go to the text with our questions, ready to see how the text will respond. In *The Practice of Preaching* Paul Scott Wilson gives a list of thirty-five questions we can ask as we engage with a text.[10] Here are a few that are particularly helpful, especially if you don't have time for all thirty-five:

- Read and reread the text on your own. Close your eyes and picture its events or the events surrounding the author or receivers, relying on clues that the text actually offers. You might even pray the text, thinking about each detail. Look in the text for things you may not have noticed before.

- What is puzzling in this text? What questions does it raise?
- What parallels exist between this passage and others?
- What happens; what is the plot or movement of thought?
- What hopeful action is God performing in the text?
- What does this tell us about who we are? Who God is?

Wilson invites us into a posture of humility before the text. The text does not serve us, we serve God's purpose through how we engage the text. Asking questions reminds us that we don't know everything. Some of us have been reading or teaching Scripture for years, and it can be so tempting to turn back to answers we've found before, which can leave us bored with the passage because we do not expect the text to say anything we haven't heard before. But if we come every week with questions, we don't approach the text assuming we already know what it says. We are allowing the text to surprise us. We are approaching the text with the humility of one who knows that the Chief Agent of our preaching is not us! We go to the text eager to hear what God has to say.

Episcopal priest, teacher and author Barbara Brown Taylor describes the experience well:

> Every preacher has a different routine for preparing a sermon. My own begins with a long sitting spell with an open Bible in my lap, as I read and read and read the text. What I am hunting for is the God in it, God for me and for my congregation at this particular moment in time. I am waiting to be addressed by the text by my own name, to be called out by it so that I look back at my human situation and see it from a new perspective, one that is more like

God's. . . . It is a process of discovery, in which I run the
charged rod of God's word over the body of my own experience and wait to see where the sparks will fly. . . . The
process of discovery begins with the text. Whether I like it
or not, I approach it believing that God is in it and I com-
mence the long, careful discipline of panning for gold.
There are translations to be compared, words to be studied,
and puzzles to be solved. What is "corban"? How much is a
talent? Where was Emmaus? More important, what did this
passage mean to the one who first wrote it down? I am not
free to pluck it out and use it in my own design. It has its
own integrity. It is part of someone else's design, and the
respectful preacher will work to discern its original meaning
before imposing any other on it. . . . It is a time of patient
and impatient waiting for the stirring of the Holy Spirit, that
bright bird upon whose brooding the sermon depends.[11]

Both Wilson and Taylor remind us that we don't know everything when we sit down to read a text. There is something fresh
here, even if we have preached on this passage many times
before. What is God saying to us and to our congregation today?
How can we slow down our own thoughts long enough to listen?

A SERMON IS NOT A "CHRISTIAN SPEECH"

After preaching through a topical series, a colleague remarked
to me, "I feel like I've spent six weeks telling them what I think
about these different topics. It was exhausting to try and preach
that way, and not very interesting."

Scripture, on the other hand, is fascinating and confusing and
messy. It is very interesting, but preaching from it faithfully
takes effort. Because of this, it can be so easy to drift into
Christian speeches instead of sermons. A Christian speech is a

spoken address on a particular topic that may or may not refer to Scripture. A message on dating is a Christian speech, for example, or "Five Ways to Manage Your Money." When people hear a Christian speech, the chief agent of change is often the person hearing the speech—"I really need to get my [money/sex life/children/marriage/devotional life] in order."

A sermon is an oral event in which the speaker humbles him- or herself before the grand narrative of Scripture and, after seeking to understand what God is up to in a particular passage, invites the hearers to know God more. A sermon says, "This is how God acted in this passage, and he is acting in our lives in a similar way right now! Today! Isn't that great?" When people hear a sermon, God changes them—whether they like it or not. (More on this in chapter two.)

Lots of people give

> **A sermon is an oral event in which the speaker humbles him- or herself before the grand narrative of Scripture and, after seeking to understand what God is up to in a particular passage, invites the hearers to know God more.**

advice, and many give it a spiritual shine. And, honestly, many of them are professionals with more time and resources than most local preachers will ever have. What makes Christian preaching different from spiritual advice? As Christian preachers, we root our words in the grand narrative of Scripture. We love the story that changes lives.

That's the difference. We actually believe this story changes lives. We've seen it happen. Marriages are restored, alcoholics get sober and stingy people become generous—all because of the gospel. As long-time Calvin Theological Seminary homiletics professor Sidney Greidanus writes, "That power is not some magical force in the words themselves but is the power of God whose word it is, for the gospel 'is the power of God for salvation to everyone who has faith' (Romans 1:16)."[12]

The Bible is not just a story that happened long ago. It's a portrait of a God who is alive and active now. When we preach, we are showing people who God is, what he does, how he moves, and we are teaching them that the more we know Scripture, the better we will recognize our God.

Christians believe the triune God speaks through Scripture in unique ways when compared with other literature. The Bible holds a special place in the library of the world's books because it is the only one God has spoken and continues to speak through. This does not mean God utters decrees in audible ways when people read the Bible. It means God the Holy Spirit uses the words of Scripture to inspire, comfort, instruct and convict people through both Bible reading and sermons that open up its meanings to those who hear.

GO DEEP

One earnest young seminarian returned from her summer placement and stopped by to chat with me about her preaching. The church she had been assigned to serve for the summer followed the Revised Common Lectionary, a collection of passages for each Sunday that includes an Old Testament reading, a New Testament reading, a Gospel lesson and a Psalm. (The lectionary is used in several denominations—Lutheran, Presbyterian, Catholic, Methodist, Episcopalian. Resources for preaching the lectionary can be found in the appendix.) This student, eager apprentice that she was, attempted to preach all four passages in her sermon every Sunday. As this was summer, the texts were during "Ordinary Time," when the lectionary, as some of you know, goes all over the map. In the church seasons of Advent or Lent the four passages often illuminate a similar theme. In the summer, however, the texts are often disconnected from each other.

"It was so hard!" she said.

"I'm sure it was," I replied. "Why did you do that?"

"Well, I kind of thought I was supposed to."

I gently suggested to her that she focus on one passage per sermon, perhaps using one of the others to reveal something more about the first, but that's it. Choose one to focus on. Have the congregation sing the Psalm for the day and use the other passages in the liturgy, but don't preach four texts at a time. That's not what the lectionary is for. And it certainly doesn't make for a more biblical sermon. In fact, trying to cover too many passages can actually make a sermon less biblical and more superficial, as the preacher dabbles here and there but never goes deep.

The same danger lurks when we need to preach a topical sermon. While topical sermons can be helpful to a congregation, and occasionally necessary, the danger in building series after series around topics is that the Bible repeatedly gets used as support for our ideas rather than the source of them. Not only does this make our sermons less biblical but it also teaches those who hear these sermons that this is how the Bible is to be used. Rather than teaching them that Scripture is to be cherished and listened to for its own sake, a regular diet of topical preaching teaches them that the Bible is a collection of pithy sayings and proof texts.

Imagine, for example, that you need to preach about money. You could write a good Christian speech about money by hop-scotching to four or five different texts. You can dabble without going deep. A more biblical sermon, and probably a more interesting one, takes one passage about money (such as 2 Cor 9) and looks hard at it, unpacking what God was up to when Paul taught about money and what God may be up to now.

An illuminating question is this: Do we read the text to prove what we want to say, or do we read the text to hear what God has to say? In the former we have an agenda and are looking for a Bible passage to match. In the second, more faithful, approach we set our agenda on the shelf and allow God to say what God will.

> **Do we read the text to prove what we want to say, or do we read the text to hear what God has to say?**

In a very practical way this affects how we plan our preaching calendars. If we plan our calendar to include a seven-part series on "How to [raise godly kids/improve your marriage/spend money well/get over your past]" the odds are high that we will page through the Bible looking for verses to bolster our case. The verses may come from various parts of Scripture, even from a few different translations, but all are chosen to help us communicate what we want to say.

In contrast, if we know that we will be preaching a series for seven weeks on the book of Colossians, we will presumably turn to the Bible for what it has to teach, and rely on the Holy Spirit for what the congregation needs to hear.

LOVE THE WORD BY SPENDING TIME WITH THOSE WHO LOVE IT

There are few things more delightful than spending time with people who love the things you love—quilting, trail running, improv. I have a friend who is fascinated by food—recipes, nutrition, cooking skills. She loves to talk with people at farmers' markets and in kitchen stores. She loves to see whether she can take a classic recipe and make it vegan. When she went to a weekend conference about food and nutrition, she was in her element—hanging out with people who loved what she loved.

For those of us who preach, Scripture can become a means to an end. We read it in order to mine it, to find a gem that sparkles enough to capture the attention of the congregation for that week. But when our approach to Scripture moves away from love and toward utilitarianism, we need to learn to love the Story again. Like my food-loving friend, we need to spend time with people who love the Story as much as we do (or once did).

If you find that your love of the Word is fading, spend time with a new convert, a Bible study group or an aged saint. New converts are incredibly curious about the Word and are waking up to the Spirit's work in their lives. Their enthusiasm about the stories of Scripture is contagious. Just recently a student sat down in my office with his Bible full of sticky notes. He had written down a list of questions about Scripture. He was new to faith and eager to learn. For an hour we sat and flipped through the Bible, talking and learning together. It was pure joy. He reminded me of the power of Scripture to transform a life.

A small group of people gathered around the Word can also be inspiring. It's amazing how the Spirit can use one passage to speak differently to each person and allow everyone in the room to understand not only the passage but also God and each other more deeply as a result of time spent in the Word. It is especially helpful if you, the pastor, do not need to lead the group! Some pastors gather together weekly for a conversation about their preaching texts. Others have parishioners study their preaching passage with them over lunch. (We'll talk more about this in the last chapter.) Listening to others say what they find interesting or troubling in a passage is often very helpful as we think about how to preach the text well.

And spending time with wise saints is priceless. Before she died, my grandmother lost the eyesight necessary to read—a great loss for someone with a house full of books. She was given a small audio Bible and dedicated herself to listening to the entire thing. When she was done, she said to me, "Now I'll listen to it again!" When we were together, we spoke about what she was listening to and what God was teaching her, and what I was reading and how God was using it in my life. At ninety-six, she loved the Word and inspired me to love it too.

Our great invitation as preachers of the Word is to love the Word—passionately, zealously, wisely, deeply—through our preaching. When we stay in love with the Word, when we dwell with the Word, when we ask questions of the Word, these practices lead us back to the Bible over and over, week after week, and inspire our own eagerness: "Now I get to preach it again!"

two

God-Centered Preaching

Luke and Erica crossed the parking lot holding hands. "That sermon gave me a lot to think about," Erica said. "I never thought about my work as a calling." Erica was the manager of a popular local restaurant. "I just thought of it as a job." Luke nodded. Erica was quiet for a moment and then said, "But I'm not sure of the link between calling and God. That was a great talk on calling—like, it was a really interesting lecture on a topic, but he didn't say much about God. I mean, did God call me to work at the Bistro? How would I know?"

"You're right," Luke began. "That was a thoughtful twenty-five minutes on the idea of calling, but I'm not sure how God fit into it."

Erica pulled out her notes. She scanned through the list:

1. God calls his people.

2. Calling relies on your gifts and stretches your abilities.

3. You are where you are for a reason.

4. You need to work hard at your calling.

"Other than the first point, he never mentioned God."

"I think that's a problem," Luke said, laughing. "I'm pretty sure a sermon has to mention God!"

Help Them See

This may seem obvious, but our sermons should mention God. In fact, our sermons should do more than just *mention* God. They should be all about God: who God is, what he has done, what he is doing, what he will do. When we speak about God, our words should create in our hearers a deeper desire to know and love God more.

Maybe you know people who are "birders": people who love to observe birds. When birders spend hours watching birds dive and fly, they don't just look at birds, they *study* birds. They examine pictures of birds so they can tell a yellow-throated warbler from a yellow-rumped warbler. They listen to recordings of bird calls so that when they hear a chirp they can identify the bird. They can tell whether a large bird is a crow or a hawk or an eagle from a far distance just by watching its wings flap. They enjoy discussing markings, molting and male-female color patterns. If you ever step outside with a birder, it's only a matter of time before she says, "Oh! There's a Swainson's thrush!"[1] And even if she's seen that very same bird only an hour earlier, there is still a note of delight in her voice at spotting something she enjoys so much.

When we preach, we teach people how to spot God. Every sermon is another lesson in how we can see God, hear God and know God. We are the leaders of the tour, wearing the large pair of binoculars around our necks, telling the group to look over here or up there, or asking them to stay quiet so we can listen carefully for the still, small voice.

When we preach, we teach people how to spot God.

Just as birders study books and images to know what they are looking for, our study of Scripture teaches us what to look for. Scripture tells us how others have identified God: Where has he been? What did he do? How did he sound? What did he look like? Reading the story of Achan may teach us how God responds to disobedience. Preaching on the annunciation may reveal how God can interrupt any life. Studying the Genesis story of Joseph teaches God's sovereignty even in seasons of waiting. Each story in Scripture teaches us how to spot God. As we prepare our sermons, one question we need to consider is, What does this passage teach us about God?

God or god?

Have you ever had your image drawn at a fair? The artist draws a caricature of you, making your freckles stand out, emphasizing the curve of your nose or giving you enormous teeth. The final image looks a little like you, but it's oddly distorted and usually funny. For many of our people, the image they have of God is a caricature. They emphasize his kindness at the expense of his justice, or they enlarge his compassion and minimize his wrath. Some even reduce his power or diminish his love.

Sociologist Christian Smith and his associates interviewed hundreds of young Americans about God.[2] He discovered that the god they describe is not the God of Scripture. They describe a caricature. The god they envision is someone who exists in order to make them feel better, and when they do not feel better, that god has let them down. To put it simply, the god they are looking for is not God.

Smith calls this caricature "moralistic therapeutic deism."[3] Here are the basic tenets:

1. A god exists who created and ordered the world and watches over human life on earth.

2. God wants people to be good, nice and fair to each other, as taught in the Bible and by most world religions.

3. The central goal of life is to be happy and to feel good about oneself.

4. God does not need to be particularly involved in one's life except when God is needed to resolve a problem.

5. Good people go to heaven when they die.

Many people in our congregations (particularly in North America) have this same understanding of God: if I do good things and live a good life, God should ensure that my life is good and that hardship does not come my way. The idea that God, as the Westminster Confession states, is "most just and terrible in his judgments; hating all sin, and who will by no means clear the guilty," is not the god they believe in.[4] Instead of being repentant of their sin and grateful for salvation, the result is that many Christians believe they are pretty good people and God owes them a pretty good life.

As Smith writes,

> This is not a religion of repentance from sin, of keeping the Sabbath, of living as a servant of sovereign divinity, of steadfastly saying one's prayers, of faithfully observing high holy days, of building character through suffering, of basking in God's love and grace, of spending oneself in gratitude and love for the cause of social justice, et cetera. Rather, what appears to be the actually dominant religion among U.S. teenagers is centrally about feeling good, happy, secure, at peace. It is about attaining subjective well-being, being able to resolve problems, and getting along amiably with other people.[5]

If we use our example of birding, this common perception of God is as close to the real thing as Woodstock of the *Peanuts* comic strip is to a real bird. Many of our people are looking for a god who does not exist. Worse than that, the god they are looking for is anemic and uninspiring. He does very little for them and asks for even less.

Who would want to worship that god?

When we preach about God—the God of Scripture, the God who is holy and hates sin, the God who pursues his people, the God who sent his Son to die, the God who sends his Spirit to empower— we are correcting their images of a false god and inviting them into a

> **Many of our people are looking for a god who does not exist.**

relationship with the true God, a God of justice and mercy, a God of grace and truth, a God who is always working to bring life out of death. This is a God who is less interested in our personal happiness than in our Christian formation (consider all the martyred apostles). Preaching about the real God, the triune God, is exciting. When we preach about God, we are showing our people who God really is, not who we would like him to be.

The United States Secret Service is part of the Department of the Treasury, and so one branch of the service seeks out counterfeiters, people who are trying to produce fake American currency. In their training for this area, officers are trained to spot counterfeit money by first studying the real thing: the color of the print, the weave of the paper, the lines in the faces of the people on the bills. The trainers know that once an officer knows all of the intimate details of a real $20 bill, he or she will easily be able to spot a forgery. The same thing applies to preaching. Our preaching must show people who the real God is, in every last true detail, so that when heresies and frauds pop up they will be able to spot them.

When we preach about the true God, our congregants will also develop a more resilient faith. If someone believes in a god whose purpose is for that person to be happy and to feel good about him- or herself, that person will quickly become angry with a god who allows bad things to happen. Elizabeth Corrie, director of the Youth Theological Initiative at Emory University in Atlanta, warns us that this anemic gospel "can't bear the weight of deeper questions: why are my parents getting a divorce? Why did my best friend commit suicide?"[6]

We may know people who left the faith when something bad happened to them. They could not believe in a God who would allow pain to enter into their lives, and so they left. They understood suffering to be incompatible with faith. But suffering is not an anomaly in the lives of Christians. We need to remind our people that no one is exempt from pain. We need to tell the stories of people whose lives fell apart and who still believed. We need to continually point to Jesus as the necessary Redeemer for a broken world. We need to give our people the eyes they need to spot God even when life gets hard.

One way to possibly prevent this is to preach about a God who is, as the confessions say, "incomprehensible." We need to preach about a God who is beyond our understanding.

Such sermons can help people to recognize the true God, even in times of struggle and loss. This also requires regular mention of the resurrection. To sustain us when sorrows come, we need to remember that death does not have the final say. As English author and essayist Dorothy Sayers (1893–1957) writes, "God did not abolish the fact of evil: He transformed it. God did not stop the crucifixion: He rose from the dead."[7] During times of suffering, God draws near with the intent to transform what is happening from something that threatens to kill to something that brings life. God is always working to move his people from death to life. The resurrection of Jesus is the reason we preach at all, and God's regular work is to bring all of his people back to life. This is the gospel we get to preach!

We want our congregations to know God, to spot God in their lives and to point God out to others. Preaching about the one true God corrects their (and our!) false assumptions about God and shows them who God really is. Preaching toward a deeper understanding of who God is enables all of us to love God more.

GOD LANGUAGE

Using precise and theologically accurate language for God enables us to counteract some of the caricatures that people have of God. We want our sermons to draw a true picture of what God looks like. Because of this, we want to be accurate with our language. The words we use when we preach about God teach our hearers how they are to speak about God. Our *God language* shapes their God language. Because of this, we need to ensure that our language for God is both rich in beauty and theologically true.

Usually, the words we use to speak about God will be those we regularly read and hear. Just as our accents are a reflection of the language we hear around us, our God language reflects what we hear about God. Too often our vocabulary for preaching can shrink to echo our own perspective about God or our own experience of God. We then teach our hearers to look for God in the places we have seen him ourselves. While this isn't necessarily bad, it does limit our preaching about God to the words and ways we ourselves are comfortable speaking about God. Our congregations, however, include an assortment of people—the shy and the outgoing, the logical thinkers and those who wear their heart on their sleeve—and our words need to help all of them understand God.

The good news is that people have been speaking about God for millennia. Reading how others have spoken about God expands our vocabularies and teaches us new ways to see what God is up to. The more we draw from how others speak of their relationship with and experience of God, the more we can spot God's activity in the present and teach our congregations how to spot him for themselves.

To speak well about how God acts now, we are helped by using the words others have used to describe God throughout the ages. The Bible, of course, is the chief source for this language. Scripture records what God does, who God is and how his people have experienced those things.

The confessions and creeds of the church are another place to find language for God. The Belgic Confession beautifully describes God and God's work in the world. Written in 1561 by Guido de Brès in the area we now call Belgium and the Netherlands, this confession was intended to set out what Protestants believed and, hopefully, to show that they were Christians who should not be persecuted by Roman Catholics. While the second goal had mixed results (de Brès himself was martyred in 1567), the first goal was achieved so well that many churches still rely on the Belgic Confession today.

As we look for language that has been used for God, particularly in the confessions or creeds, we will notice that some of these words are not found in our everyday language. My colleague Scott Hoezee suggests "using the 5 cent synonym right after the 25 cent term and doing this routinely week after week," as a way of caring well for our congregants and expanding their vocabulary of faith at the same time.[8] As you read these lists, think about the "5 cent synonyms" that could work in your context.

The Belgic Confession begins by stating who God is:

Article 1: The Only God

We believe in our hearts and confess with our mouths that there is a single and simple spiritual being, whom we call God—

Eternal,

incomprehensible,

invisible,

unchangeable,

infinite,

almighty;

completely wise,

just,

and good,

and the overflowing source of all good.[9]

This is an example of rich and deep God language. When we use adjectives like these to describe God, it shapes how we understand God and also how we then expect God to act in our lives. Knowing that God is incomprehensible will affect my response when I face bewildering challenges. Knowing that God is the overflowing source of all good, I can spot him when goodness breaks into my life. When our God language is nuanced and layered, it shapes how we understand God himself.

This is hard, mostly because our human nature desires to constantly remake God in our own image. We want God to look like us, think like us and share our priorities. Submitting our ideas about God to the truth that is God is a reminder that we are not God. Painful but important.

Another church document, the Westminster Confession, reminds us that we are not God and God is not like us. Originally written in 1646 for the Church of England, it was also adopted by the Church of Scotland and has since been used by Presbyterian churches around the world.

Submitting our ideas about God to the truth that is God is a reminder that we are not God.

This is how the Westminster Confession speaks of God:

> There is but one only, living, and true God, who is infinite in being and perfection, a most pure spirit, invisible, without body, parts, or passions; immutable, immense, eternal, incomprehensible, almighty, most wise, most holy, most free, most absolute, working all things according to the counsel of his own immutable and most righteous will, for his own glory; most loving, gracious, merciful, long-suffering, abundant in goodness and truth, forgiving iniquity, transgression, and sin; the rewarder of them that diligently seek him; and withal, most just, and terrible in his judgments, hating all sin, and who will by no means clear the guilty.[10]

As we read these articles of faith, we may become aware of words that we rarely use in our preaching—*most free*, for example, or *long-suffering*. It may also be the case that we become aware of things we know about God but avoid in our preaching, such as "most just, and terrible in his judgments."

If there is a word or phrase that you rarely preach, think about why that is and whether excluding it leads to a caricature of God. Perhaps you'll find that you spend a great deal of time in your sermons trying to explain God, especially in times of loss or tragedy. How would it change your preaching to remember that

God is "incomprehensible" but also "most loving"? Reading the foundational creeds and confessions of the church allows us to let our ancestors in the faith teach us again about who God is and what he has done. Rather than assuming these words are dated or musty, we trust they can ground us and stretch us just as they have done for preachers for centuries.

Consider as well the God language that is typical in your community and how it may need to be stretched. If your community usually speaks of God as powerful, you may also need to teach that God is gentle or patient. If your community is looking for God only in positive answers to prayer, you may need to preach on how God reveals himself when he says no.

The words we sing also influence our God language. Many of our songs are unitarian, mentioning God but not naming Father, Son or Holy Spirit. The lyrics in contemporary Christian worship songs are often written to evoke a feeling rather than to teach theology. But the words still teach! What does singing about God's love "like a hurricane and I am the tree" teach us about God?[11] If God's love is like a hurricane—a word associated with destruction and loss—would any of us want it? What does "like a rose trampled on the ground" tell us about Jesus?[12] That he is fragile? Or beautiful?

Here too older hymns may have words that need a bit of explanation. "Interposed his precious blood" from "Come, Thou Fount of Every Blessing" may be a line you want to unpack before you sing it. The line is rich but *interposed* isn't a word we use often. When I worship next to a new or not-yet believer, I read the song lyrics through their eyes and realize how many of the songs we sing have stained-glass words (words used only in church) that my new-to-church friends probably do not understand. How can we teach new believers proper and helpful language for God as we sing?

Reviewing words associated with each member of the Trinity also helps our God language to be precise. Though the entire Trinity is involved in God's external acts, we wouldn't say that the Holy Spirit is crucified, for example, or that the Son descended on Pentecost. But we do say that all persons of the Trinity were present at creation, and that the words used to describe God in the confessions apply to each person of the Trinity.

To spark our imaginations, here are some of the words drawn from Scripture, creeds and confessions that are used to describe each member of the Trinity.

Words usually associated with God the Father.

- create
- uphold
- rule
- provide

- turn evil to our good
- commission
- call

The Belgic Confession says, "The Father is the cause, origin, and source of all things, visible as well as invisible."[13]

Words usually associated with God the Son. This list is much longer than that of Father and Spirit. The Gospels, of course, give us many ways in which Jesus is described and many ways in which he describes himself. The length of the list does not imply that we should speak twice as often about Jesus as the other two persons of the Trinity, although every Christian sermon should speak of Jesus.

- heal
- teach
- convict
- prophesy
- die

- rise
- intercede
- pray
- suffer
- sacrifice

- empty self
- servant
- crucified
- descended to hell
- ascended to heaven
- human
- divine
- flesh
- incarnate
- Immanuel
- tempted
- saves
- way
- truth
- life
- gentle
- humble
- Bread of Life
- Living Water
- Resurrection and the Life
- Light of the World
- Good Shepherd
- Head of the church
- Bridegroom
- seated at the right hand of the Father
- Judge
- anointed
- prophet
- priest
- King
- Lord

The Belgic Confession says, "The Son is the Word, the Wisdom and the image of the Father."[14]

Words usually associated with God the Holy Spirit.

- empower
- equip
- descend
- convict
- help
- groan
- Giver of Life
- assures of eternal life
- makes us wholeheartedly willing and ready from now on to live for him
- makes us share in Christ and all his blessings

- comforts us
- remains with us forever
- produces faith in our hearts
- confirms faith through the sacraments
- grafts us into Christ
- poured out on God's people

The Belgic Confession says, "The Holy Spirit is the eternal power and might, proceeding from the Father and the Son."[15] And "The Holy Spirit kindles in our hearts a true faith that embraces Jesus Christ, with all his merits, and makes him its own, and no longer looks for anything apart from him."[16]

Reading through these words can invite us to stretch our language and our imaginations to help our hearers look for God in fresh ways.

Too often we may also use the word *God* generically and only mention God the Son when preaching from the Gospels, or only refer to God the Holy Spirit on Pentecost. Seeing the attributes of each member reminds us to incorporate the distinct roles of all three persons of the Trinity in our sermons. A sermon on a hard text in Judges, for example, may make us long for Jesus, who will return to make all things new, or make us grateful for the work of the Spirit, who groans for us. A Gospel sermon on Jesus' ministry of healing could note that Jesus' ministry redeems the curse, allowing the created work of God the Father to flourish once again, or could remind us that even when we are not healed, the Spirit is our Comforter.

> Seeing the attributes of each member reminds us to incorporate the distinct roles of all three persons of the Trinity in our sermons.

PRACTICALLY SPEAKING

The great joy of preaching is that we get to introduce people to the triune God! The God who creates, redeems and sustains this world is active in our lives today, just as he has been since before time began. When we preach, we draw from ancient descriptions of who God is and how he works, so we can point to a God who is acting now just as he always has. This is why we preach: to introduce people to a God who loves them and show them how he is loving them today.

So how do we do this? Let's use the sermon Luke and Erica mentioned in the story at the beginning of this chapter, the sermon on calling. Erica had listed these points in her notes:

1. God calls his people.

2. Calling relies on your gifts and stretches your abilities.

3. You are where you are for a reason.

4. You need to work hard at your calling.

This is a good outline, including important points on the idea of calling. But as Luke and Erica said, the sermon doesn't talk a lot about God. To improve this sermon, we should ask, What can we teach about God as we teach about calling? What do people need to understand about God if they are really going to understand calling?

The sermon was based on the call of Abram recorded in Genesis 12. God called Abram to leave where he was and go to the place God would show him. So what if we redesigned the outline to make God the actor and not us?

1. God can call anyone at any time: "Now the LORD said to Abram, 'Go . . .'"

2. God's call will stretch you: "to the land that I will show you."

3. God's call has the big picture in mind: "I will make of you a great nation."

Now God is the active agent in each point. The sermon is about God, not about an idea. For each point of the sermon our thoughts are brought back to God and how he works.

One temptation when preaching sermons from the Hebrew Scriptures is to use generic God language and forget to mention Jesus or the Holy Spirit. Christian preachers should strive to mention Jesus and the resurrection life made possible by the Holy Spirit in some way in every sermon. I often tell my students that we can't preach sermons that would be acceptable in a synagogue, because the resurrection of Jesus and the empowerment of the Spirit change everything. We preach the Old Testament as people who know how the story continues.

So for this sermon we want to be clear, especially in the third point, that God's big picture includes Jesus Christ's coming and the Holy Spirit's filling. He calls Abram to move because he is going to use Abram to start a nation that will eventually include a young woman named Mary, who will give birth to the Son of God himself.

As I have mentioned earlier, a sermon isn't just review of what God did once. It reveals that if God acted that way then, we can look for him to act in a similar way now. For each point in this sermon, our goal would be to show how God interacted with Abram and then show how God interacts with us. The outline would look something like this:

1. God can call anyone at any time: "Now the LORD said to Abram, 'Go . . .'"

2. God can call you at any time. (This point could include how we listen to God, perhaps teaching about how the Holy Spirit speaks through the words of Scripture and the communion of saints as well as through our own hearts to call us to something new.)

3. God's call stretches Abram: "to the land that I will show you."

4. God's call will stretch you. (Perhaps this point gives an example of people whom your church knows and how they were stretched. It may be a good idea to give varying examples—from adopting a child to volunteering at a food pantry to moving to another country.)

5. God's call on Abram has the big picture in mind: "I will make of you a great nation."

6. God's call on your life has the big picture in mind. (This point should emphasize that God's call on our lives often results in Christ being formed in us and in our potential to teach about Christ to others. We may want to ask the people how God is calling them to be a blessing.)

This sermon teaches people about God, how he acted toward Abram and how he acts toward us. It also reminds them of who God is—sovereign and all powerful, with a plan for each of us that he is carrying through to completion. In so doing it brings people into contact with the living God, which is the goal of preaching. The sermon also serves as a counternarrative to "moralistic therapeutic deism," because the sermon reminds people that God's call on our lives doesn't always feel good; in fact, the call of God may stretch us in uncomfortable ways.

> **A sermon brings people into contact with the living God, which is the goal of preaching.**

The sermon ends by reminding everyone that God's big picture includes them and also includes a plan for redeeming the world. The sermon points toward Jesus as the fulfillment of God's plan in Abram's life and in ours. In this way it is distinctly Christian. When the sermon incorporates the Holy Spirit as communicator of the will of God and the one who equips us with gifts for service, we have a sermon that is trinitarian, aligned with God's revelation of himself.

God Spotting

One of the best things about being a pastor is that we have a front-row seat to the activity of God in our people's lives. We can watch God heal, convict, convert and help in a wide variety of situations. We see how he shows up when people aren't expecting him, and how he provides daily bread when someone needs to get through another day.

Untrained people can walk through a forest of birds and not know what to look for or listen to. But the birds are there waiting to be found! People need to be taught where to look and how to listen. It's the same with God—he can be seen and heard, but many of us need someone to show us where to look and how to listen.

Teaching our people where to look and how to listen is our calling as preachers. We get to say, "Look! There he is!" and see the delight in people's eyes when they too spot him. Really, why would anyone want a different job?

Preach about God. There's nothing better.

three

Grace-full Preaching

"Don't Preach at Me!"

I once had a seminary student say to me, "I can't wait to start preaching so I can tell people what to do!" That's the popular conception of preaching: someone standing in front telling other people what to do. The assumption of inadequacy is built into that understanding of the word *preach*: "You are not living the way I (or maybe God) want you to live, so I need to tell you all the ways you are disappointing me (and maybe God) and give you ways to improve." We can picture the furrowed brow and wagging finger.

Who would want to listen to that?

But so often this is exactly what we do when we preach. We are subtle, most of us. We don't usually wag our fingers at our congregants and tell them all of the ways they are messing up. But how often do our sermons end with ways our people can improve?

- If your relationship with God is important to you, you will make a commitment to talk to him every day.

- If you want to take your discipleship to the next level, you will start incorporating service into your life.

- Our children deserve the best this church can give them. What can you do to invest in the lives of our children?
- Isn't it time for your money to be invested in eternity?

Too often, we make following Jesus sound burdensome.

A student plunked down in the chair next to me. "My boyfriend broke up with me," she began. "It wasn't a good relationship, and now that it's over I realized how far I am from God. I really want to get close to God again."

I consoled her over the breakup and commended her desire to grow closer to God. "Tell me," I asked her, "what do people usually do to get close to God?" She was easily able to list the usual spiritual disciplines: read Scripture, pray, go to church. "You know all the right answers," I said. "What's keeping you from doing them?"

"They sound like so much work," she said. "I don't know if I have it in me to do the work."

Many of the people we preach to know the right answers. Some of us have the joy of discipling new believers who don't know how to follow Jesus. In either case, we invite them to read Scripture, serve, pray, worship. Why don't they do it? Because we make it sound like such work!

As one middle-age dad said to me, "I come into church carrying all the burdens of the week. I have a long list of things I need to do at home, at work, as a spouse or a friend or a parent. I am well aware of where I am not measuring up. When I go to church I long to hear comfort and assurance, something that will lighten my load. What I get instead are more things for my to-do list—pray more, read more, serve more. Here are five ways to be a better parent. Three ways to evangelize at work. I leave thinking that I am simply not enough. It's exhausting."

Becoming the Congregational Parent

If we are honest, our desire to tell our congregants what to do often arises out of our own anxieties. We spend hours reading and studying Scripture every week, we scan articles about leadership and attend conferences that give us ideals of what the local congregation could be. Then we look out on our church on Sunday morning and see all that is not happening. Leon was supposed to call someone to check the leak on the water heater. Kate was going to write up the minutes of the evangelism committee. It's been weeks since you asked the worship committee to think about an outdoor Easter service for the neighborhood and you've heard nothing.

> **If we are honest, our desire to tell our congregants what to do often arises out of our own anxieties.**

At times like these we feel like the mom who walks into the house to find the shoes and boots scattered in the breezeway, coats thrown on the floor and backpacks blocking the door. She wants to yell, "How many times have I told you to put away your things when you get home from school?!"

"How many times have I told you to be kind to visitors?"

"How many times have I told you to set up a budget?"

"How many times have I told you to pray every day?"

The temptation is to place ourselves in the position of congregational parent rather than pastor. By doing this we are saying that we are the adults, we have our acts together, we have outgrown all the immature behaviors we see in our church, and we have the right and the authority to tell them how to live.

When we place ourselves in the role of congregational parent, we are communicating to our parishioners that we do not see what they *are* doing, we only see what they *aren't* doing. Or we only see them doing the things we don't want them to do. We are telling them that we do not accept them where they are.

A distance grows between us and our hearers. Our perception of them and their lives becomes small, anemic and sad. And then our views of our own lives and the choices we make can become twisted. We can actually come to believe that if everyone lived as we are living, the church would be lively and healthy. Then whatever burden the sermon contains (pray more, serve more, improve your parenting) gets placed on them and not on us. We assume that we are already doing it.

A second danger in being the congregational parent is that the relationships between us and our congregants can become transactional. Instead of loving them because it's our calling and our job, we unintentionally communicate to them that we will love them more if they do what we are asking them to do: "I am doing all of these things for you as your pastor, therefore you should do these things for me." "If you do the things I am asking of you, I will like you more than I like the people who don't do what I ask." "If you want to get me to like you, here are the ways." Then it affects how they see each other: "The preacher likes me because I [recycle, tithe, volunteer] more than you."

If this goes on too long, the transactional relationship does not stay pastor–people. People translate it to God–people. They come to believe that their relationship with God is also one of give and take. "If I do what God asks, God will do what I ask." "If I am obedient, God will love me more." "If I live a good life, God will protect me from hardship." "I know how to earn my way into God's affection." "I'm on God's good side."

Remember the Gospel?

The gospel, thanks be to God, is not about a transactional relationship. The gospel tells of a God who so loves us that he sent his only Son to save us. This is important: we do nothing; God does everything. "While we still were sinners," Paul writes in Romans 5:8, "Christ died for us."

When we preach as if we could work to make God like us more, we are selling out the gospel. As best-selling Christian author Philip Yancey puts it, "We need to let it soak in that there is nothing we can do to make God love us more . . . and nothing we can do to make God love us less."[1] God loves us. It is nutty, crazy, go-to-the-ends-of-the-earth-for-you love. And that's exactly what God did. God in Christ died for us, went to hell for us, rose for us and wants nothing more than to be with us forever. All of the things we have done and will do wrong, all of our sins, our shortcomings, our addictions and our depravity itself are done away with in the cross of Christ:

> My sin, oh, the bliss of this glorious thought!
> My sin, not in part but the whole
> Is nailed to the cross, and I bear it no more,
> Praise the Lord, praise the Lord, O my soul![2]

Whenever we preach anything that makes our hearers think they need to work harder to make God (or us) love them more, we are not preaching the gospel.

Preaching Grace

We need to preach grace.

Grace says that God did it all and we *can* do nothing. Not that we don't have to do anything, but that we actually can't. All our righteousness is like filthy rags, says Isaiah 64:6. We are actually incapable of contributing to our salvation. As Paul writes, "For by grace you have been saved through faith, and this is not your own doing; it is the gift of God" (Eph 2:8).

So if every sermon needs to preach the good news of a gospel of grace, does every sermon end the same way? "Well, God loves you and there's nothing you can do to lose that love so, you know, just go do whatever this week."

If we are preaching grace, where is the application? How do we call people to holy living or tithing or kindness or commitment if we preach grace? How do we call them away from believing in moralistic therapeutic deism?

To preach grace isn't to let people off the hook. To preach grace is not to tolerate poor behavior, in ourselves or in others. To preach grace is to remind people that we get to live differently because of what God has done. Living a holy life is not a burden. Obeying God's will for our lives is not to check things off yet another to-do list. Living as God invites us to live is a gift! Living as a disciple of Jesus Christ is to live in response to God's grace.

> To preach grace is to remind people that we get to live differently because of what God has done.

A friend of mine donated bone marrow to someone he didn't know. My friend had signed up through Be the Match, a program that seeks to collect donor samples to match with patients who need transplants. My friend received a letter telling him that he was a match, and he responded. The donation was successfully accepted in the stranger's bones, and the stranger's cancer went into remission as a result. After a donation through Be the Match, there is a waiting period before the recipient can communicate with the donor (if the donor has agreed in advance to this). As soon as the waiting period was up, my friend received a beautiful letter from the man who received his donated marrow, thanking him for saving his life. The now-healthy man wanted to meet my friend and his family.

They met, and my friend and his family were overwhelmed by

the sheer gratitude of the man, his wife and his friends. The man's best friend offered them his cabin in Georgia, telling my friend, "You saved the life of my best friend. I will always be grateful. Whenever you want the cabin, it's yours."

Why the overwhelming gratitude? Because they had lived with the threat of death. If a match had not been found, or if my friend had declined to donate, that man would have died. Death wasn't a possibility; without the donation death was guaranteed.

Preach Sin

This may sound odd, but the gospel of life is less compelling if we don't actually believe in the threat of death. If we don't actually believe in hell. If we don't actually believe that without Christ we would live in eternal misery. If we don't believe we are sinners, we don't believe we need grace.

To preach a robust belief in grace means we also need to preach a robust doctrine of sin.

Author and theologian Cornelius Plantinga puts it this way:

> To speak of sin without grace is to minimize the resurrection of Jesus Christ, the fruit of the Spirit, and the hope of shalom. But to speak of grace without sin is surely no better. To do this is to trivialize the cross of Jesus Christ, to skate past all the struggling by good people down the ages to forgive, accept, and rehabilitate sinners, including themselves, and therefore to cheapen the grace of God that always comes to us with blood on it. . . . In short, for the Christian church (even in its recently popular seeker services) to ignore, euphemize, or otherwise mute the lethal reality of sin is to cut the nerve of the gospel. For the sober truth is that without full disclosure on sin, the gospel of grace becomes impertinent, unnecessary, and finally uninteresting.[3]

We need to remember how close we are to death to understand the immensity of the gift of life. We need to know the pain of our sin to know the relief of God's grace.

To disappoint the student who wanted to "tell people what to do," when we preach we remind people how close they were to death, how God's gift of his Son saved them and how we all live grateful lives as a result. We don't tell them what to do; we tell them what God has done.

PRACTICAL GRACE

What does this actually look like? How do we preach grace-filled sermons instead of offering to-do lists?

The key is in how we frame the human response to divine grace. Our response is not one of task or burden, but one of joy in getting to join God in the work he is already doing in the world.

Michael Le Roy, president of Calvin College, tells the story of painting with his father and his son. He and his father were preparing to paint a room and Michael's son, Dana, then a small boy, offered to help. Michael was reluctant, but his father (just like a grandparent) readily agreed. He gave the boy a brush and while the adults worked steadily to cover the walls, Dana had a small area that was his. Although Dana hardly contributed to the project, and now admits he may well have been a nuisance, what he remembers is the pride he felt at helping the grownups paint the room.

That's how we preach grace-full responses to the sermon: we are the little ones who get to help! Does God need us involved in the project? Not really. But does he want us involved? Absolutely. God's chosen way of building the kingdom is precisely by using us as his hands and feet. We *get* to work with God toward the coming of his kingdom!

So in our sermons, we suggest responses as ways for people

to partner with God. As University of Toronto preaching professor Paul Scott Wilson writes, "The purpose of the sermon is to invite people into faith; the purpose of faith is service to the gospel of Jesus Christ. From faith issues action; thus the sermon points listeners toward their active ministries in the world."[4]

Pointing the listeners toward their active ministries in the world is much more enjoyable than telling them what to do. As preachers this move places us in a posture of humility, as our people are partnering with God and taking direction from him, rather than obeying us as the congregational parent. In our sermons we call them to pay attention to how God is moving in their families, dorms, workplaces, friendships, cities or nation and invite them to join him in that work. The language changes from "this is what you need to do" to "this is what we get to do."

> **The language changes from "this is what you need to do" to "this is what we get to do."**

We move from language like this:

- Now we will . . .
- We can change because . . .
- You can make your life better by . . .

To language like this:

- Because Jesus has given us this authority, we are now able to . . .
- As the Spirit works within us, we can . . .
- Because God never lets go, we live our lives . . .

To illustrate further, let's take the examples from the very beginning of this chapter and rewrite them so the response is animated by grace. We'll take the basic intent of the "Congregational

Parent Version" and rewrite it into a grace-filled version. You'll notice that the grace-filled versions are longer, as they include practical examples.

Congregational parent version: If your relationship with God is important to you, you will make a commitment to talk to him every day.

Grace-filled version: God's love for you is like a grandparent's for his nine-year-old granddaughter. When you call, his whole face lights up. He can't wait to hear what you have to say. And when you hang up, he can't wait for you to call again, just so he can hear your voice. No matter what you say, what you'll hear him say every time is that he loves you.

Congregational parent version: If you want to take your discipleship to the next level, you will start incorporating service into your life.

Grace-filled version: Paul was clear that the Holy Spirit has poured out his gifts on the church. The Holy Spirit has poured out his gifts on you! On me! And his work doesn't end with giving us the gifts. The Holy Spirit is eager to be with us when we use them. He will show you the person who needs you to care for him or her, or the family who could use a meal, or the young parents who could really use a night out. If you can repair a car or care for a child or write a song, the Holy Spirit can use you! Ask for him to guide you to the place where you can serve. And then stand back and watch him get ready to work through you. It may not be flashy, it may not draw attention from anyone else, but you'll know and he'll know. And the body of Christ will benefit.

Congregational parent version: Our children deserve the best this church can give them. What can you do to invest in the lives of our children?

Grace-filled version: Jesus welcomed little children into his arms and blessed them. And he wants to keep blessing them through us. Your arms are the arms of Jesus. What little person needs your arms to give him a hug, or your fingers to show her how to knit, or your hands to help build on the service trip? Jesus is still blessing little ones and this time we get to help.

Congregational parent version: Isn't it time that your money was invested in eternity?

Grace-filled version: Our money can feel so personal. We don't ask each other how much we make; we don't ask how much we spend or save. We don't know how much someone else gives. How we use our money can be private, but it's not personal. It's communal. God gave it to each of us for the good of each other, for the good of the church, for the good of the world. God has a million ideas of what to do with our money, and all of them are better than ours. What would happen if we gave it all to him?

Once we understand what God in Christ has done for us, says Wilson, there is an

excitement to obedience. . . . Such excitement arises from being enlisted by God and empowered by the Holy Spirit to accomplish God's will of vulnerable, self-giving love for others. We depend on God to fulfill our calling. God is the actor bringing forth God's purposes in which we have an important part to play. [The work we do] is not a task but a privilege, honor and opportunity.[5]

Responding to the Sermon in the Service

Some worshiping communities are using creative ways to have listeners respond in worship after they hear the sermon. Whether through song, prayer, physical movement or artistic expression, a well-chosen response can secure the ideas of the sermons in the lives of the hearers.

Most liturgies, whether they are formal or not, have a song that follows the sermon. If we have preached a message of grace, singing words that build on that idea and name us as partners in God's work is a strong way to fortify the sermon. Song lyrics matter. When we choose the song that follows a message, we can choose one that builds on or echoes the grace-filled message of the sermon. This allows the congregation to give voice to what God is doing among them. If you have talented poets or musicians in your church, consider asking one of them to take a well-known hymn tune and write a new verse that reflects the message of the sermon.

In some of our traditions the sermon is always followed by the sacrament of Communion, so the response happens at the Table—the clearest expression of God's grace to his people. When we preach on Sundays that include the sacrament, we "set the table" with our preaching. On these days we want to be sure that nothing we preach undermines the grace expressed in the Table. The bread and the cup are signs of what God has provided. As one liturgy says,

> We come not because we ought, but because we may,
>   not because we are righteous, but because we are penitent,
>   not because we are strong, but because we are weak,
>   not because we are whole, but because we are broken.[6]

A physical response, such as eating the bread and drinking the cup, allows congregants a way to act out what has been preached.

Some worship services and some worship spaces allow us to think creatively about how we want our worshipers to respond, even on days when we do not have the sacrament. Do we want them to come forward? To offer something? To write? To speak? To be silent?

A way to get your mind to think in fresh ways about possible responses to your message is to employ the five senses: What does the grace of God smell like? What does the love of God sound like? What does the mercy of God taste like? Imagining possibilities like this can move your preaching from the cerebral to the incarnational: How can our bodies receive and respond to God's grace?

Here are a few suggestions that may prompt your own (and your worship team's) ideas.

- *Baptism*: In celebrating baptism, your church could employ the deep-rooted tradition of sprinkling the entire congregation with water. Older children could carry small branches dipped in water and while walking the aisles of the church gently shake the water on worshipers. The theme of the sermon would emphasize that God's power of baptism extends through our entire lives.

  Such a sermon would include this: "Baptism isn't a sentimental moment in our lives. It's not when we felt warm and fuzzy toward God and so we were baptized. Baptism is God's action toward us, action that does not end. The power of God at work in your baptism is relentless. You are experiencing it even today."

- *Name tags*: When preaching on Paul and his new name as "slave of God," one preacher talked about how God gives all of us new names. At the end of the sermon she invited worshipers to come forward, take a blank name tag from the

Communion table and use one of the markers provided to write down a name God had given them.

The sermon ended with, "What name is God giving you today? Forgiven? Beloved? Child of mine? When you have that name, come up and write it on a tag and wear it. Then when you get home, you may want to stick the name tag on your calendar, your computer or your bathroom mirror to remind you that just like Paul, when we come to Christ we get a new name. God gives us a fresh start."

- *Dumpsters*: Some churches or Christian communities rent dumpsters and place them in public areas so that during the season of Lent people can literally throw away the things keeping them enslaved to sin. Dumpsters have collected everything from flash drives of pornography to CDs, hoodies from old boyfriends, boxes that have been taped closed, letters of confession, video game cartridges and junk food.

  Your sermon could invite worshipers into this practice: "You may not think you can really give up this sin. And in your own strength, you probably can't. But with God's power, you can. God is giving you what you need to throw away the sin that so easily entangles and to run with perseverance the race he's marked out for you."

- *Bowls of water*: After a sermon on purity, worshipers could be invited to come forward to the bowls of water set up in the front of the sanctuary and to wash their hands as a sign of their dedication to living holy lives. The bowls could be set on stools with towels draped over the top rung. People could wash their hands and dry them.

  The sermon could set up such a response this way: "One of the great promises of God is that he takes our sins away 'as far as the east is from the west,' and he forgets them.

They are washed away. Because of Christ's sacrifice for us, God sees us as pure. We wash our hands to remember the purity that is ours in Christ and to remember that God helps us to live as his holy people."

Practices such as these give people an immediate way to respond to the message, and the action is done communally. We respond together to the grace that is preached.

DISTINCTLY CHRISTIAN

To preach grace is to preach the gospel of Jesus Christ. As Philip Yancey points out, "The Buddhist eight-fold path, the Hindu doctrine of karma, the Jewish covenant, and Muslim code of law—each of these offers a way to earn approval. Only Christianity dares to make God's love unconditional."[7]

This is what preachers do: we speak of God's unconditional love. God himself—the mighty One, the spinner of galaxies, the Word made flesh—is eager to partner with us in revealing the wideness of his mercy and the sufficiency of his grace. So preach grace. Preach it often and preach it well, and watch how God gets to work.

four

Compelling Preaching

Marie sat across from her pastor. They had met at a coffee shop to review the agenda for a committee she chaired, but that work was done. Now Pastor Mike had asked her, casually, "May I ask what you think about my preaching? You're involved in church, and I appreciate your advice on so many things. I'd love to get your perspective on this."

Marie sat quietly for a second, weighing her options. She'd been a member of the church for a long time. She'd heard many preachers over the years. She could tell Mike that his preaching was just fine. She learned a lot, and she loved his humor—she could simply tell him that. But it wasn't always fine. Sometimes it was frustrating. Marie had worked with Mike for a few years and she knew she could trust him. And as an older member of the congregation she felt responsible. So she took a breath, looked him in the eye and after telling him that she learned a lot and loved his humor, she said, "But, I'm not always sure of your point. I mean, you say a lot of interesting things, and they all tie in to the passage somehow, but I sometimes walk away unsure of what you really wanted us to know. I also find it hard to remember any of it during the week—there's too much I'm trying to recall, and I end up with nothing."

Pastor Mike leaned in, interested, so Marie continued. "Think about it this way: you hand us a lot of things to carry. We first get the passage and then an idea about the language, and then an idea about the author, and then something else about our church as an illustration, and then another idea about the culture of that day—and by the time you're done, our hands are full of an assortment of things that seem to have nothing to do with each other. It's like handing someone a pumpkin, a map of Chicago and a kitchen chair. Each of those things is interesting, but we don't know which of those things is most important or what they have to do with each other, and we can't hold them all at the same time."

As Pastor Mike walked back to church from the coffee shop, he thought about what Marie had said. She was very kind, but also very clear. His sermons were well-researched and full of information, but lacked focus. He wondered why this was. As he opened the door to his office, he saw papers and books for next Sunday's sermon spread across his desk. He looked at the wall of bookshelves, full of commentaries on every book of the Bible and resources on the culture of the ancient Middle East. His computer was loaded with the latest language software. He found it all captivating, but he wondered if this was what was behind Marie's concern.

Information Overload

If you're like most preachers, a survey of your bookshelves reveals rows of commentaries, thick books on theology, the dog-eared books you read in Bible college or seminary, and an assortment of Bibles, including some in Hebrew or Greek. When we are studying a text, many of us go all in: our desks are covered in different books, with Post-it Notes scattered throughout and various sections highlighted. We scan our shelves or search online for one more nugget of information. We have an assortment of apps open on our tablets and click back and forth, gleaning whatever we can.

Part of the reason we love preaching is because we get to learn. We get to read great scholarship and unpack forms of speech and learn what a denarius is. We can search preaching websites and lectionary databases. We can find an enormous amount of material on every single passage of Scripture, much of which we find endlessly fascinating.

And we want to share this with our parishioners. All of it. We want them to know how this passage influenced Luther, how Augustine read it or what Eugene Peterson's translation reveals. We want to connect to this pop song, reference this movie and mention this cool thing we read on social media. We want them to know all the interesting factoids we have learned over the course of the week. We show up on Sunday brimming with information, and while we preach we are so enamored with the stuff we're saying we don't realize that most of our listeners are making grocery lists in their heads. As prominent twentieth-century American preacher Harry Emerson Fosdick (1878–1969) pointed out, "Only the preacher proceeds still upon the idea that folk come to church desperately anxious to discover what happened to the Jebusites."[1]

One of the challenges to sermon clarity is the vast quantity of information we take in when we research a text and our hesitation to leave any of it out of the sermon. Because we find it all very interesting, we think that our people will too. But they don't. Every new piece of information is another idea they are trying to hold. Eventually, they get tired of collecting the new things you're handing them and stop listening.

Structural Issues

Sitting at his desk, Pastor Mike reviewed his outline for Sunday's sermon. It looked like this:

1. Idea 1

    a. Support for idea 1

    b. Greek grammar about idea 1

    c. Quote about idea 1

2. Idea 2

    a. Interesting cultural note about idea 2

    b. Old Testament reference for idea 2

    c. Funny story about idea 2

3. Idea 3

    a. Application of idea 3

    b. Theological implications of idea 3

    c. Quote about idea 3

4. Summary of Ideas 1, 2, 3

It made good sense when he wrote it, but when he tallied up the different pieces of information—the various things he was asking his listeners to hold—he counted at least a dozen.

Mike had been taught to write research papers in this way, as many of us have. State the point, support the point and then move on to the next point. This works when we are writing a paper, because a reader can flip back a page at any time and remember what the idea for each section was. A reader can also see paragraphs and subheadings visually, which helps to categorize the information. But when we use this style for an oral presentation, it can be very hard to follow. Without a copy of the document in front of them, our hearers can't figure out how the quote about idea 1 connects to idea 2, which comes right after it, or how the funny story about idea 2 serves as a bridge to idea 3, and because it's not a paper they can't flip back to remind themselves of what was already said or see the paragraph breaks that signal the next section.

When people listen, they are seeking order. Our parishioners are listening for a structure like this:

$$1 \rightarrow 2 \rightarrow 3 \rightarrow 4 \rightarrow 5$$

They want to know how 1 leads to 2 leads to 3. (This doesn't mean that the sermon has this many points. This is an example of how each element of the sermon [idea, illustration, quote, story] flows easily from the previous point and easily into the next point.)

As long-time Dallas Seminary and Gordon-Conwell Theological Seminary preaching professor Haddon Robinson writes,

> Three or four points not related to a more inclusive point do not make a message; they make three or four sermonettes all preached at one time. Reuel L. Howe listened to hundreds of taped sermons, held discussions with [laity], and concluded that the people in the pew "complain almost unanimously that sermons often contain too many ideas." That may not be an accurate observation. Sermons seldom fail because they have too many ideas; more often they fail because they deal with unrelated ideas.[2]

Because of this, Robinson, along with many others, stresses that a sermon should have one big idea.

Think of a sermon as a cascading waterfall in which the same water flows from one shelf to the next. Each fall is slightly different (larger, smaller, quicker, slower), but the same water is moving throughout. The water is the big idea of the sermon. Each step along the way illuminates that one big idea rather than introducing a new one.

In the story that opened this chapter, Marie is asking Mike to give his congregation one thing to hold, and then to explain the nuance and beauty of that one thing.

ASK THE MOST IMPORTANT QUESTION

When we preachers begin to study the passage for the week, we have a swarm of things buzzing around in our heads: last night's worship committee meeting, the funeral next week, our kid who was up sick last night, the dinner conversation with friends, and of course the things that are supposed to be there: the text, its language, its history, its author, its intent, its interpretation through the years and even whether or not we like it. The swarm buzzes and hums, growing louder the more we study. The whole process can be quite maddening.

How can we calm the swarm? How can we move from the flurry of thoughts to one clear idea?

We may find it helpful to begin our process by asking this question: What is God doing in this passage? There are lots of reasons to read and study Scripture (form, structure, language, culture), but our congregation isn't interested in most of those questions. Their big question is this: What is God doing in my life? A great way to figure out what God is doing *now* is to learn how he worked *then*: with Abraham or Miriam or Isaiah or Luke. When we answer the question, What is God doing in this passage? we can more easily answer the question, What is God doing in my life?

> When we answer the question, What is God doing in this passage? we can more easily answer the question, What is God doing in my life?

So when we go to our text for the week, we seek to answer, What is God doing in this passage? There are, of course, many possibilities: Is Jesus teaching by way of a parable? Did God do something worthy of praise? Is the Holy Spirit empowering people? Is God punishing someone?

Sometimes God is obviously active: Jesus heals someone or the Holy Spirit directs or the triune God answers a prayer for a child. Then the central focus of our sermon is the central focus of the passage: Jesus wants his disciples to be salt and light, therefore Jesus wants us to be salt and light. Or God answered Hannah's prayer in God's timing, therefore God will answer our prayers in God's timing.

Let's look at an example. If we are preaching on Matthew 5:13-16 (the passage from the Sermon on the Mount about salt and light), the answer to the question, What is God doing in this passage? is this: Jesus is telling his disciples to let their light shine. Jesus is encouraging (You are the light of the world!) and challenging (Let your light shine!) his followers. To build on this idea, a sermon structure based on this passage could look like this:

Introduction: Teaching on the reasons why salt and light were so precious and necessary in the first century.

1. The world of the disciples longed for people who were as valuable as salt and light.

2. Our world still longs for people who are as valuable as salt and light. (What does our world need? What are the rare elements that people long for?)

3. Jesus empowers his disciples to be those kinds of people. (What would it look like in their culture for Jesus to empower them to be salt and light?)

4. Jesus empowers us to be those kinds of people. (What would it look like in our culture for Jesus to empower us to be salt and light?)[3]

The sermon is about one big idea: Jesus empowers his disciples to be salt and light. The four moves of the sermon explore this idea and what it meant then and what it means now. The sermon is simple and clear, and answers the questions (1) What is God doing in this passage? and (2) What is God doing in my life?

When the Question Is Hard to Answer

But what about the many passages of Scripture in which God (Father, Son or Holy Spirit) isn't even mentioned? There are many passages in which someone else (e.g., Paul) tells someone to do something, but God seems uninvolved. How can we bring God into a passage when he's not doing anything obvious?

To explore possibilities for these situations, let's look at two types of texts that can be particularly challenging this way. First, Psalm 84, a psalm of praise.

> How lovely is your dwelling place,
>   O Lord of hosts!
> My soul longs, indeed it faints
>   for the courts of the Lord;
> my heart and my flesh sing for joy
>   to the living God.
>
> Even the sparrow finds a home,
>   and the swallow a nest for herself,
>   where she may lay her young,
> at your altars, O Lord of hosts,
>   my King and my God.
> Happy are those who live in your house,
>   ever singing your praise. *Selah*
>
> Happy are those whose strength is in you,
>   in whose heart are the highways to Zion.
> As they go through the valley of Baca
>   they make it a place of springs;
>   the early rain also covers it with pools.

They go from strength to strength;
    the God of gods will be seen in Zion.

O Lord God of hosts, hear my prayer;
    give ear, O God of Jacob! *Selah*
Behold our shield, O God;
    look on the face of your anointed.

For a day in your courts is better
    than a thousand elsewhere.
I would rather be a doorkeeper in the house of my God
    than live in the tents of wickedness.
For the Lord God is a sun and shield;
    he bestows favor and honor.
No good thing does the Lord withhold
    from those who walk uprightly.
O Lord of hosts,
    happy is everyone who trusts in you.

In this psalm God isn't doing anything obvious. The psalmist seems very happy that he has finally arrived at the temple, but as for God, he seems to be a passive recipient. What is God up to in this passage?

If we look at the first section, the psalmist is focusing on physical space. He is thinking about the literal temple. He may even be looking at the temple and seeing a bird's nest up in a corner. He experiences the temple as a good place to be; one could even say it's a safe place. There is a sense of joy and relief and even nesting associated with the temple. And why is this? Because this is a place where God has provided these things. The safety and rest available at the temple are so apparent even the birds can see it.

In the second section the writer is thinking about those who are coming to the temple from other places. They are so eager for the journey that even as they come, they make better the places they travel through: the valley of Baca, which was a literal desert and a place of tears, becomes a "place of springs"—the sign of life![4] The pilgrims are going from "strength to strength," because the pilgrimage to the temple is a journey of joy. Before they even get there they are infused with strength.

In the final section, the psalmist names what God does: "The Lord God is a sun and shield; / he bestows favor and honor. / No good thing does the Lord withhold / from those who walk uprightly." These words are a summary of what the psalmist has been saying throughout the psalm: the Lord is generous in giving good things (safety, rest, strength) to his people, and all of those things are seen in his house, the temple.

What does God do in this passage? Focusing the sermon on one main idea—God's generous care for his people, seen in his house—will be more compelling to preach and to hear than a complex breakdown of the language and cultural elements at play in the passage.

Let's try it again with a passage from James in which God is not immediately obvious:

> You must understand this, my beloved: let everyone be quick to listen, slow to speak, slow to anger; for your anger does not produce God's righteousness. Therefore rid yourselves of all sordidness and rank growth of wickedness, and welcome with meekness the implanted word that has the power to save your souls.
>
> But be doers of the word, and not merely hearers who deceive themselves. For if any are hearers of the word and not doers, they are like those who look at themselves in a mirror; for they look at themselves and, on going away, immediately forget what they were like. But those who look

into the perfect law, the law of liberty, and persevere, being not hearers who forget but doers who act—they will be blessed in their doing.

If any think they are religious, and do not bridle their tongues but deceive their hearts, their religion is worthless. Religion that is pure and undefiled before God, the Father, is this: to care for orphans and widows in their distress, and to keep oneself unstained by the world. (Jas 1:19-27)

In this passage James, like our big brother, is instructing us on how to live. On first read there is much he is asking us to do, and not a lot that God is doing. In fact, it seems we have quite a bit to do!

A good question to ask is why? Why is James asking us to step up? Maybe the reason is found in that first sentence: our anger does not produce God's righteousness. God seems invested in our righteousness. Reading on, it seems that God has implanted his word in us in order to save us. And in the last paragraph James says there is religion that is pure and undefiled before God, which is to care for those who have no one to care for them and to keep oneself unstained. A strong theme in this passage is righteousness, which James also names as purity or remaining undefiled. There is also the promise that those who do the word and don't just hear it will be blessed.

So we ask, Who wants our righteousness? Who will bless us when our lives are marked by doing as well as hearing? God, of course. What does God do in this passage? One possible answer would be that God blesses righteousness.

PUT THE SERMON IN ONE SENTENCE

Now that you've determined what God is up to in this passage, the next step is to put that into one sentence. This forces us to be clear. We can't get away with fuzzy thinking if we need to say the entire sermon in a sentence.

For example, one sentence about Psalm 84 could be this: The psalmist recounts his deep joy and relief at worshiping in the temple, celebrates that others are able to pilgrimage in strength, and points to God as the one who bestows favor and honor. All of those things are true and faithful to the text, but each one introduces a different idea. That sentence gives the congregation several things to hold.

A way to counteract this inclination is to put the sermon in one sentence with God (Father, Son, Holy Spirit) as the first word. We also want the sentence to be simple, without commas, and to use a strong action verb if at all possible.

Putting the sermon in one sentence and making God the subject of the sentence forces us to clarify the most important point of the passage. Knowing that, here's another attempt at a single sentence about Psalm 84: God gives his people the gift of his house (safety, rest, a place to nest). Is the psalmist joyful about this? Yes. Does he celebrate the pilgrimage of others? Yes. But is the psalm about the psalmist? No. The psalm praises God for what God has given. When we answer the question, What is God doing in this passage? with, God gives his people the gift of his house (safety, rest, a place to nest), we can build a sermon on one clear idea.

An additional challenge with this psalm is that the literal temple is no more. The gift of the house God gave to his people is gone. What does he give us now? Many passages link the Jewish temple with the church, the body of Christ. If we think of all that we are given in the church, we can see that these things are the same as those given to God's people through the temple. God is still generous toward his people, so the clear idea of the psalm finds application in contemporary life.

A helpful organizing structure to outline sermons and keep God as the focus can be found in Wilson's *Four Pages of the Sermon*. He encourages preachers to order sermons as (1) Trouble in the Text (what need or problem was presented then?), (2) Trouble in the World (what does that same need or problem look like now?), (3) Grace in the Text (what was God doing then?) and (4) Grace in the World (what is God doing now?).[5]

If we use Wilson's model, the structure could look something like this:

1. The psalmist longs for God's house, a place to nest.

2. We long for God's house, a place to nest.

3. God generously gives his house (the temple) to his people.

4. God generously gives his house (the church) to his people.

We can see how the clarity of the one idea allows the rest of the sermon to flow from one element to the next. There won't be extended tangents about what kind of bird the psalmist was referring to or seven minutes on the Valley of Baca. What will come is a clear sermon about the need in the text and how God answered it, as well as the same need in our lives and how God satisfies it today. This is also why we use the same verb in section three and section four: God does now what he did then.

Let's try this with James 1. Our answer to the question, What is God doing in this passage? could be this one sentence: God blesses righteousness. Of course, we want to avoid preaching about a God who gives us a good life in response to our righteousness. In the fullest sense *blessing* means anything that brings about our formation as disciples. This doesn't mean things always go the way we want. With that acknowledged, a possible sermon structure looks like this (again, using Wilson's *Four Pages* model):

1. The readers of James were tempted to not live righteously.

2. We are tempted to not live righteously.

3. God blesses their righteousness.

4. God blesses our righteousness.

The epistle of James is a dense book. In this one short section alone there are many ideas and imperative verbs. Whittling this section to one sentence seems to leave so much out. But moving from homiletical clutter to sermon clarity demands that we make hard cuts. We also know that if we were to write a sermon on this passage in the future, the outline may not look exactly the same. The Holy Spirit may lead us to look at another aspect of God's work in this passage and apply it to our context in a different way. The important thing in any case is to place ourselves under the authority of the Word and Spirit, and seek to preach what the Word says as the Spirit leads. We also help our listeners if even before we read the text we say something like "There is so much in this passage, and we could look at many aspects of what James is saying here. Today, however, we will be focused on the idea of righteousness."

Kill Your Darlings

Many passages of Scripture have an assortment of ideas flowing through them. From this one passage in James we could write a sermon about anger, listening, speech, the law, the word, widows, orphans, meekness or the world. To give our sermons clarity we need to do the hard work of picking one idea and letting the rest, for now, stay in our study.

It's not just the multilayered ideas in the text that force us to make hard choices. We have all had those moments preparing a sermon when we come up with just the right idea, the right turn of phrase or the perfect illustration, and then we realize it does not fit our major theme. We are tempted to keep it in because it is so brilliant, makes us look so funny or will please so many people. But if the idea, phrase or illustration does not promote the main idea, we need to delete it.

Writers refer to this as "killing your darlings" (a phrase that is direct, but a bit distasteful). Writing teacher Arthur Quiller-Couch first used the phrase in his 1913–1914 Cambridge lectures *On the Art of Writing*. In his 1914 lecture "On Style," he said, "If you here require a practical rule of me, I will present you with this: 'Whenever you feel an impulse to perpetrate a piece of exceptionally fine writing, obey it—whole-heartedly—and delete it before sending your manuscript to press. *Murder your darlings*.'"[6]

Mr. Quiller-Couch knew well the temptation to wax on needlessly because the author (or preacher!) was enjoying it so much. But for a sermon to be clear, we need to be ruthless about including only ideas, phrases or illustrations that illuminate the main idea. If it doesn't talk about the particular thing we've identified that God is up to in this passage, we need to leave it out.

SPEAKING CLEARLY ON TOPICS

We aren't always preaching sermons, though. Sometimes we are asked to speak to a group on a particular topic. We may use a text as a springboard, but we aren't going to go deep into the text because it doesn't fit the occasion. Maybe there are three points we hope to make, and they are all related to the main idea but aren't really related to each other.

Let's say that you are speaking to a group of Christian leaders at the start of their season (academic year, sales year or church year). You've been asked to give them some ideas about leadership. Leadership is a vast topic, and you have twenty-two minutes.

You begin to think about what's captured your attention recently and find yourself pondering Psalm 57, especially verse 8:

"Awake, my soul!" You start thinking about the connection between an awake soul and leadership.[7] You jot down a few ideas: leaders shouldn't be lone rangers, leaders shouldn't have sleepy souls, leaders should know that grief and loss aren't the end of the story. You ponder illustrations about being awake, about being connected to others, about what makes a soul sleepy, about people who have gone through deep grief and testify to how that season grew their souls.

Your outline may look like this:

Awake, my soul! What keeps us awake, that is, attentive to God?

　　1. Leaders shouldn't be lone rangers.

　　2. Leaders need to avoid having sleepy souls.

　　3. Leaders don't need to fear grief or loss.

Each point is important, and for each point you have a story. But for your listeners there isn't an obvious link from 1 to 2 to 3, nor is there a link from each of them to the main idea: "Awake, my soul."

One way to draw disparate points together is through alliteration: using the same letter for each point. Alliteration helps people connect disparate thoughts.

The outline could then look like this:

How to have an awake soul:

　　1. Don't be alone.

　　2. Don't be asleep.

　　3. Don't be afraid.

Alliteration makes it much easier for people to follow the speech, and it would be easy to connect these points to the main point. When delivering the speech, you could repeat the points as you add them, allowing the clarity to come through not only in content but also in delivery. But we can take this one step further.

When I was a pool lifeguard, I observed that when someone was running on the deck (a dangerous move) and I yelled, "No running!" the person would often take a few more quick steps before slowing down. You could see the person thinking, *Am I running? Is the lifeguard yelling at me?* But if I yelled, "Walk!" the person would stop almost immediately. The positive command worked much more effectively than the negative one: the person knew that he or she was not walking and was being asked to do so right away. The same often goes for public speaking. Inviting our hearers to *do* something is easier for them to remember (and to act on) than telling them to *not* do something.

> **Inviting our hearers to *do* something is easier for them to remember (and to act on) than telling them to *not* do something.**

So let's spin this outline into three positive commands.

Awake, my soul! Leaders are

1. Reliant on others

2. Revived by God

3. Resilient in trouble

Now your ideas are shaped into a clear and positive message that will be easy to follow and, as a bonus, easy for you to remember.

Making an outline easy to follow and positive to hear takes more time and energy, but now your listeners can track easily with you and the main idea and the supporting points will be very clear in their minds.

Always Learning

Pastor Mike sat across from Marie in the same coffee shop where they had met three months earlier. After their last conversation Mike had worked hard on making his sermons clear and compelling. It had been difficult for him to leave some insights in his study, and there were some long afternoons of wrestling with a text to discover what God was doing there. But he had already picked up that his parishioners were listening differently.

For one sermon he used an outline consisting of three Bs (something he'd never done before), and later that week someone referenced it casually in an education committee meeting to illustrate a point. In another sermon he repeated his God sentence almost as a refrain (God calls us to live out our faith so that he can bless us), and a middle-school student repeated it back to him when she was being challenged for her faith at school. Mike was surprised and pleased.

Marie had noticed too. "I walk away with one big idea to chew on for the week," she said to him. "It's really helpful. When you read the text now, I am already eager for what you are going to teach us. I know you aren't going to swamp us with information, but you're going to pull out the best nugget and let us study it together. It's fun."

Pastor Mike smiled. "Let's do this again in three months," he said. "These conversations are making me a better preacher."

five

Imaginative Preaching

The Power of Story

My stepsons come barging in the door after seeing a movie with their dad. They are laughing and talking and quoting lines from the movie as they scour the cupboards for snacks.

"How was the movie?"

"It was really good! So funny."

Then I ask this question: "What was it about?"

I usually get a play-by-play of the story line, with one of them talking over the other to clarify a point in the plot. They tell me about the actors and the cars and the funny parts. They tell me who won in the end and if this one was better than the other one that was kind of like this one but starred that other guy. All of this is said through mouthfuls of cheddar and sour cream potato chips, of course.

Never, in all the times they have told me about movies, has either one ever looked at me and said, "I can't remember. There was this guy, and maybe he was a detective or something, and he had a car. Something blew up. I don't know."

They always know. They can always remember. They can always tell me.

That's the power of a story. We can remember a movie because someone is telling us a story. The story begins with people who need something, or something happens to them, or there is the promise of love, the threat of global extinction or an epic battle between good and evil. The story unfolds as the characters respond to whatever comes their way. A good story draws us in because we want to know how it turns out: Did the accused commit the crime? Do the aliens wipe out life on earth? Does the girl find love? Find out this Christmas in a theater near you!

Our challenge as preachers is that almost everyone who listens to us knows how the story turns out. God is in the still, small voice. The boy kills the giant. Jesus heals the blind man. Thomas professes faith. Paul, once again, tells people what to do. Yawn. Why should our people keep listening if they know how this is going to end? There is a problem. God solves it. Take the offering.

We need to create tension, or we need to acknowledge the tension that is already there. Because although most of our hearers know how the Bible stories turn out, they don't know how their stories are turning out. They can't read to the end of their books. All of us—preachers and pew sitters—listen to the words of the Bible and think, *Is it true? Does it matter? Will it happen for me?*

> **All of us—preachers and pew sitters—listen to the words of the Bible and think, *Is it true? Does it matter? Will it happen for me?***

That's the tension. Is this truth true for me? Is this God really God for me? Are my sins really forgiven, and how would I know? Does a life of obedience really matter when it's costing me so much?

And there is our hook. Everyone walks into church hoping, praying, begging for something to be said or sung that will help them, comfort them, assure them and sometimes challenge them, convict them or push them. To put it simply: they want to see themselves in the story.

PUT THEM IN THE STORY:
ILLUSTRATIONS THAT CONNECT

This is why illustrations matter. Illustrations help to place us in the story. But illustrations that invite us in need to be something we can actually imagine. Most of us did not fight Nazis in World War II. If you ask us to place ourselves in that story, we will always imagine ourselves as the hero—hiding Jews in our basement or standing up to the SS or giving bread to the hungry soldier from the other side. But many of us can more realistically imagine ourselves fighting with a sibling over the remote control or, in later years, fighting about where the extended family will have the reunion, or who should tell Dad it's time to stop driving, or who gets the dining room table when parents have died. We won't imagine ourselves the hero in these stories because we probably haven't been. What we need in a story about our siblings is some idea about what to do next—what it would really look like for us to be like Christ, not in some French village in 1942 but in the family room today or on the phone tomorrow.

Because we know that illustrations help our hearers place themselves in the story, we preachers can spend a great deal of time searching for the perfect illustration: the story that ties to the Scripture passage, is just the right length and moves us easily to the next point. This is why there are books of illustrations available to buy and websites eager for you to subscribe to their ideas. But canned illustrations usually taste that way: the essence of a good story, but lacking in color and tang.[1]

The strongest illustrations are drawn from the life of the church itself. If you start a sentence with "This week in the Bible study, Ben mentioned . . ." or "Nancy, the chair of our deacons, invited me to join her on a benevolence visit this week, and . . ." heads are going to go up. People are going to pay attention. Ben said something interesting in Bible study? What happened on the benevolence visit? (Or what is a deacon? What is a benevolence visit?)

Suddenly the life of the church has made it into the sermon. Someone was paying attention to things that happen every week. This wasn't a once-in-a-lifetime event. Bible study happens every week. Deacons visit people all the time. This was regular life being called out as an example of kingdom living. The illustration wasn't theoretical, distant or abstract. It was personal, relatable, accessible and relevant. That gets people's attention.

This also means *we* need to pay attention. If you have read and studied your text early in the week, think of yourself as flypaper for the rest of that week: anything that could link this text to the lives of these people should stick to you. An exchange with the server at lunch. A magazine article on change management. A song on the radio. Another passage of Scripture. A great quote on social media. As the week goes on, write these things down. Even if it is only remotely connected to what you're preaching about, record it. You never know how the Spirit may use it.

One important note: *Always ask permission.* If Ben says something in Bible study that catches your attention, mention it to him afterward and see if he's okay with you using it and if he wants credit. Say something like, "I loved what you said about verse 5. I may be able to use that on Sunday—would it be okay if I mentioned your name?" Don't promise that you're going to use the illustration. We all know that what looks perfect on Wednesday morning may not fit when we are finishing the sermon on Saturday night.

We also know that some brilliant illustrations hit us at 6 a.m. Sunday morning, and we don't always have time to check with the person before we preach. But if they don't know you are going to use them, *don't use them.* The use of others in illustrations is an opportunity for us as pastors to care well for people. We want them to look good in illustrations, and we want them to feel safe at church. Respect their wishes if they do not want to be used, or offer to change their name or the details of the event if that makes them more amenable to the idea. But if they decline, honor that. Think of your use of illustrations as an opportunity to build trust with your congregation.

Beyond Illustrations: Other Ways to Make It Memorable

Say that again: the power of refrain. Did you know that the draft of Dr. Martin Luther King Jr.'s famous speech in front of the Lincoln Memorial was actually titled "Normalcy—Never Again"? Why is it remembered differently? Because of the refrain. "I have a dream" is repeated eight times in the seventeen-minute speech. People on the scene say that gospel singer Mahalia Jackson was stepping off the stage as King was stepping on. "Tell 'em about the dream, Martin," she called to him.[2] And he did, improvising much of the speech in the moment but returning to the phrase "I have a dream."

As any of us who have attempted to memorize anything know, repetition helps us remember. Whether it's the grocery list or the names of the twelve apostles, repeating something locks it into our memories. The same applies to sermons. If we hear someone say, "It's Friday, but . . ." many of us will say, "Sunday's comin'!" because we have heard or read Tony Campolo's sermon of that title.[3]

Most people aren't taking notes while we preach. They are simply listening. In this context a refrain can tie a sermon together and help them remember the main idea of the sermon, even if they don't join in saying the refrain. While some of our congregations would appreciate the opportunity to talk back, some of them would be completely flummoxed if we asked them to say anything during the sermon. But they will pay attention if *you* say it.

So as you're preparing your message, think about the big idea, as Haddon Robinson would say.[4] What's the main message of your sermon? Is there a refrain that encapsulates the idea? Or is there a line from a song that could be repeated during the sermon, and then the entire song could be sung following the sermon? Or perhaps a line from the passage could be learned by the whole congregation as they listen. The goal of a refrain isn't that it's catchy or clever, the goal of a refrain is that when people repeat it later in the week, they can remember the point of the sermon.

Show and tell: use a prop. Remember show and tell from elementary school? One day each week students in the class were invited to bring an object from home and take turns showing their object to the class and telling the class about it. (Of course, the day that someone else had his mom bring in their litter of new puppies was the day you forgot to bring anything and you had to make up a story about a pencil you found in your desk.)

Using a prop in a sermon is a bit more involved than show and tell. You do have an object, and you do want to tell about it, but you want that object in some way to serve as a link between the passage of Scripture and its interpretation or application. You don't want to bring in a turtle for novelty's sake, but to use the turtle to teach about how God is our fortress, about the armor of God or about basking in God's glory. The object should illuminate the passage.

Because we want the prop to be helpful throughout the sermon, the prop needs to tie clearly to the Scripture passage. When people see the object later in the week in their own lives, we want them to remember what was preached and why. The goal of a prop is the same as the goal of an illustration or a refrain: when people think of it later in the week they should be able to remember the point of the sermon. Because of this, props should be simple and, if possible, something that most people use or see every day. If you preach to a community of farmers, talk about a piece of farm equipment (be sure your references are up to date, as contemporary farm equipment in North America is incredibly sophisticated). If you have a number of kids in sports, consider using a ball, a net or a whistle. One of my colleagues asked an artist in the congregation to paint a picture throughout the message and then showed it to the congregation at the end of her sermon. Another person used a backpack to represent the burdens we carry. Because I work at a school where the mascot is a knight named Joust, I had Joust come and stand with me as I preached on the armor of God.

Don't work too hard at finding a prop. Because they are not a requirement of preaching, you can simply let the ideas come as they do. Here again, if you go through your week like flypaper, you'll be ready for a good idea to stick to you. Allow the prop to support the message, but don't force it. If the prop works great for your opening illustration but halfway through preparing the sermon you find yourself working too hard to make it relevant to your sermon's conclusion, then the prop is driving the sermon and you'll have to "kill your darling."

When you do have a prop, use it throughout the message. Don't use it as part of an opening illustration and set it aside, or have it sitting in view of everyone for the whole sermon only to be used at the conclusion. You can have the prop sitting out at the beginning and then use it for the last two-thirds of your sermon. This creates curiosity and a bit of tension that helps people listen (*Why is there a birdcage on the stage? Why is she wearing a backpack?*).

You also don't want the prop to distract from the message. A colleague was preaching to college students on the cognitive dissonance of the resurrection. At a certain point in the sermon he was holding a small, lit candle. He then popped the lit candle in his mouth and ate it. He compared the dissonance of eating a candle to the disbelief of the disciples about the resurrection. However, the students were so stunned that he had eaten a candle that he could hardly get through the rest of the sermon because they were so distracted—did he really just eat a lit candle? (The candle was a chunk of apple and the wick was a sliver of almond stuck into the top.)

As distractions go, also remember the words of comedian W. C. Fields: "Never work with children or animals." He knew they would steal the show. And as any of us who has offered a children's message can attest, they steal the worship service as well. So unless you know that the child or animal in question will do exactly as you wish (in front of everyone, under pressure), avoid using children or animals as sermonic help.

Use props on occasion and avoid building up an expectation that there will be a prop in every sermon. That can trap us into turning every sermon into a gimmick.

Logical order: ABCs and 123s. One older homiletic tradition is "three points and a poem." A preacher would name his three points, calling out, "My first point," "The second point" and "My final point," before concluding the entire sermon neatly with a verse from a hymn. While other forms for preaching may be more commonly used now, this form does have its benefits; one of them is that a sermon with a clearly logical order can be easy to remember.

If you say at the beginning of the message that today's sermon will have three points that start with the letter B, some listeners will be relieved because the goal is clear and there is a way to reach it: no surprises, no twists in the plot, three points, the letter B— go! Some of our hearers love the order of the three-point sermon, especially when they are explicitly told that it is coming. For some of us this may feel like we are showing our hand too early. We want to keep people listening all way through. However, it's important to remember that our listeners have different learning styles, and for some the logical order allows them to learn best. (For others, however, the alliterative style is too simplistic and will turn them off. Be wise about how often you use it.)

Using logical order is a tool that works especially well when we want our congregation to learn something. You may not need them to *feel* something or *realize* something in this sermon, but you really want them to *understand* something. If that's the case, a sermon would benefit from having three or four points that allow them to understand and retain information. This is especially good when you are preaching about doctrine. You want your listeners to learn about baptism or atonement or the omnipotence of God in such a way that it sticks with them. If you can have three points with the same letter, great. If the four points spell out a word, fine. But don't work too hard to bend the sermon to match the alliteration or the word. We've all known the frustration of spending way too long trying to come up with just the right word when the rest of the sermon could use more attention. Remember that all of the points need to illuminate one single idea. Each point can't be a fresh thought on a separate topic (see chap. 4).

Image. A colleague of mine began a sermon with the story of Susan Ford, the daughter of President Gerald R. Ford, who held her senior prom at the White House. My colleague told us about the invitations sent out, the excitement at the high school, the preparations everyone made and how everyone dressed up and used their best manners. He spun the story so well that all of us wanted to be invited to the White House prom. He then turned that anticipation toward the wedding feast of the Lamb. His image was a special party, and his point was that no one would turn down an invitation like that. It worked: the strength of the image allows me to remember the whole sermon several years later.

An image is a repeated description of a gesture, object or event that can serve as a reference point throughout the sermon. Think of it as a prop that you invite everyone to imagine. In the previous example my colleague painted such a great picture of this party (Tuxes! Ball gowns! Great food! Music! Dancing! The president of the United States!) that we all wanted to come.

A strong image can hold a sermon together. Some Scripture passages lend themselves to great images—vines and branches, shepherds and sheep, judges and plaintiffs, potter and clay. Our work as preachers isn't as hard when we get to preach passages like these. But what happens when we preach Romans? Or Jude? Adding color to the more didactic portions of Scripture can be a challenge.

So as you read through the passage, consider the following questions:

1. If I had to draw a picture of this passage, what would it look like?

2. What colors would I use?

3. Does the passage change color, moving from dark to light?

4. Does this passage remind me of an event that has happened in my life? In the life of the church? In my city? In the world?

5. Is there something happening in the world right now that could serve as an image in this sermon (the Tour de France, a global summit, a yacht race, an election)?

6. If I had to teach this passage to eight-year-olds, how would I do it?

7. If there was one picture on the bulletin cover or on the screen that captured this sermon, what would it be?

Just as with a prop, the image should be strong enough to serve the entire sermon. We don't want to talk about Cheerios for the first point, dryer sheets for the second and golf for the third. Choose one image and pull it all the way through the sermon.[5]

MAKE IT MEMORABLE, BUT TELL THE TRUTH

Our deep desire to make a sermon memorable can lead us to make some questionable ethical choices. Once I was reviewing a student's sermon with his class, and one student noted that she really appreciated the preacher's illustration about his Uncle Jim. "Oh, I don't have an Uncle Jim," he said, "I just wanted a good story there." Stunned, I stopped the class and reminded them that our listeners demand us to be truthful: "If we invent a relative just to serve our cause, our integrity is compromised. If I can't trust you to tell me the truth in a sermon, of all places, can I trust that you're telling me the truth anytime? Can I trust that the rest of what you are preaching is true?"

Another student challenged, "But what if no one will find out?" I said, "You will know, God will know, and is 'no one will find out' ever a good reason to do anything?" The student preacher had to rewrite the sermon.

All preachers have "friends," as in, "I have a friend who was in line at the store when . . ." or "I have a friend who works in law enforcement. She said . . ." We want to tell a story without giving away an identity and without spending too much time setting it up before getting to the punch line. And most of the time we are the only people who know whether we really do have a friend who said what we just reported. This allows preachers a great deal of wiggle room to fudge facts. (I'll restate something from the introductory chapter: All stories in this book are fictional, though many come out of conversations I've had. For stories out of my own teaching, identifying details have been changed to protect the identity of the students. Whenever possible, the source has been asked prior to using his or her story.)

We need to think about these things:

- If the person mentioned were in the congregation, would she recognize herself in the sermon?

- If so, would she know I was using her in the illustration?

- If the person is mentioned by name, is the mention favorable?

- Does the story make her look good?

- If the elders asked me at our next meeting if all of my illustrations were true, could I say yes?

- Could I name the person who was in line at the store?

- Could I tell them who I know in law enforcement?

We also want to signal to the congregation that we will honor their stories. A clarification helps: "This week in the Bible study, Ben mentioned something, and I asked his permission to share it with you." The entire congregation will want to know what Ben said, and they will also learn that if you ever want to quote them you will ask first. This is a great way to increase trust across the congregation. I had one pastor in a class who said that he occasionally begins stories by saying "Long ago and far from here" so the church will know it's not about any of them. Another always uses the same names, which are not the names of anyone in her congregation, for the people in her illustrations. (Be aware that names of the characters in our illustrations signal age—"Nancy" and "Carol" are of a different generation than "Katelyn" and "Taylor." If "Nancy and Carol" are shopping, they could be buying dining room furniture. "Katelyn and Taylor" may be looking for the cheapest biochemistry textbooks.)

The goal of our illustrations is not only to make a sermon memorable but also to tell the truth. This also applies to any outside sources we use. When a good idea isn't yours, tell them. Imagine that Frederick Dale Bruner, author of an extensive Matthew commentary, is in your pew when you are preaching on that Gospel. Would he recognize his ideas, and if so would he be honored by how you used them? A simple line such as "Scholar Frederick Dale Bruner points out that . . ." alerts your hearers to the sources you are using. Another idea is to list in the bulletin or post online the commentaries or books you're relying on for a particular series. Some of us have amateur Bible

The goal of our illustrations is not only to make a sermon memorable but also to tell the truth.

scholars and future preachers in our pews who would love to know what we are using. And for all of us this provides another way to be held accountable.

When You Use Someone Else's Sermon

Every now and then you have one of those weeks. You're sick or someone dies and there are two weddings, and when you try to scrape together something for Sunday, you can't. There's nothing there. While you may be tempted to grab something off the Internet and pass it off as your own, stop. Because this is what could happen: A friend of mine (get that?) was new to town and visiting local churches, looking for a place to settle in. One Sunday he slid into a pew, scanned the liturgy and grew hopeful. He liked the order of worship, he knew many of the songs, and the people had been friendly on the way in.

When the pastor of the church stood to preach, he mentioned that he had been ill that week and thanked a few people who had filled in for him. He then read the text and began the sermon. The sermon started with a story that the preacher noted had happened to Tom Long, a well-known teacher of preaching and a fine preacher himself. What this preacher did not say was that *the entire sermon* was Tom Long's, something my friend recognized as he had heard the sermon when it was preached at a conference. Long's sermon was later transcribed and published. The preacher at this local church was presenting the sermon as if it were his own, with no mention of the true author. He even claimed that the illustrations had happened to him. My friend, disgusted, left during the next hymn and never returned to that church.

As my professor friends say to their students about plagiarism, "If you can find it online, I can find it online." If you find a sermon online and preach it as your own, it's only a matter of time before one of your parishioners stumbles across it.

So when you have a hard week, what do you do? Call the chair of your elders (or whoever has authority over your preaching and can help you). If the person you call doesn't know what kind of a week you've had, fill him or her in. Then ask if, with permission, you could preach a sermon written by someone else for this Sunday. (Maybe other people need to weigh in as well; you know your church's systems and order.) If the leader or leaders agree, on Sunday morning mention that you've been ill, thank the people that filled in, and then say, "Because of my challenging week, I wasn't able to prepare for you the way I normally do. With the elders' [board's, steering team's] permission, I'm going to be presenting a sermon written by Tom Long, a professor of preaching at Candler School of Theology." Your integrity is intact, the church leaders are in the loop and the service goes on.

CONCLUSION: MIX IT UP

There's a Sunday in every week, and many of us preach most of them. You don't want your sermons to get in a rut, and if you overuse any of the memory aids I've mentioned, your people will get tired of them. Something novel soon seems trite if it's used every week. (Another prop? Four points that all start with P?) So use a prop on occasion. Alliterate your sermon points every now and then. Even images can blur together if there is one in every sermon.

And not every sermon is going to be memorable. (There will be many we would like to forget!)

Thankfully, our calling is not to be impressive, it is to point people to God and his activity in the world. We believe that God uses the power of the preached Word to change lives. All of the tools in this chapter are nothing if they are mere gimmicks used to entertain or impress. They are to be used in the service of proclaiming the good news of Jesus Christ.

six

Contextual Preaching

Before the baptism the preacher told the story of the child's birth, long awaited by a couple who had struggled with infertility. The preacher told the story beautifully and gracefully, noting that he had permission from the couple to do so. The young mom was beaming and teary. The young dad kept taking deep breaths. The baby slept through it all. By the time the water was poured on the baby's head, tears were streaming down many cheeks.

The congregation sang a hymn, and then the preacher read the text and started the sermon. And no further mention was made of the baptism.

This holy moment, one that arose from years of prayer, one that required great faith and surrender on the part of the young parents and one that other couples in the congregation were praying for themselves, was never mentioned in the sermon. It was as if the baptism happened at not only a different event but a different church!

WHAT IS CONTEXTUAL PREACHING?

To preach contextually means preaching a sermon for these people, in this place, on this day—when the baptism has happened, when the youth group is back from their trip or when the congregation has mourned a loss. To preach contextually is to connect the preached word with the deep needs of these people at this time. Although it feels like an individual event, preaching is a really a team sport, arising from and responding to the particular needs of a particular congregation. The sermon is not a standalone piece of performance art.

Swiss theologian Karl Barth (1886–1968) is credited with saying that we need to preach with the Bible in one hand and the newspaper in the other. Contextual preaching includes the larger political and social landscape: Are your members worried about wars? The spread of disease? Friends in the Mideast? Upcoming elections?

But there is more to contextual preaching than mentioning current events. To preach contextually as the pastors of our congregations, we need to preach with the Bible in one hand and the social media feeds of our congregants in the other. If someone asked you what the worries are of your church, would you know? Do you know what they are thinking about? Or what joys happened for them this week? What challenges they encountered?

And while we can learn much from social media (who's on vacation at Yosemite, whose kid lost a tooth, whose friend is engaged), the knowledge of their hopes and fears isn't as easily gained. This is the knowledge absorbed while leaning over cups of coffee or chatting in the parking lot after a meeting. This is what we learn when we stop by the nursing home or paint a house with the youth group. In these informal conversations we learn what's on their hearts.

And this informs how we read the text for that week. To preach for your context is to take what you know about your congregation and read the text through their eyes. What do they need this sermon to address? What is happening in their lives right now that can be spoken of on Sunday morning? What hopes and fears do they carry with them as they approach the text? How can you pastor them well from the pulpit?

> **To preach for your context is to take what you know about your congregation and read the text through their eyes.**

STUDY THEM

This means that we have to know our people. We have to know their names, but we also have to know their stories. In my first months of ministry I sent a note to the students I would have in Sunday school that fall. I was curious about them and wanted to know what they were curious about. Many of them attended Christian day schools, so their knowledge of Bible and theology was pretty thorough. What would get them interested in coming to Sunday school? I had a list of ideas and asked them to choose.

After worship the following Sunday, a parent of one of those students strode up to me in the back of the church.

"What do you mean by giving them a choice?"

It took me a minute to figure out what she was referring to. "Well, I, uh . . ."

"Those kids need to know the catechism! That's what you need to teach them!" Her eyes flashed. "I don't care what they *want* to learn; this is what they *have* to learn!"

She stormed off, and I stood there unsure of what had just happened.

Thankfully, I asked my copastor about it, and he told me about her older child, a son who had wandered far from the church. "She doesn't want that to happen to her daughter," he said. "Her words came out of her worries."

It would have been so tempting for me to seethe about what she had done—in the rear of the sanctuary, in full hearing of everyone standing around—but now that I knew her story my anger and embarrassment quickly changed to compassion.

You can name the people in your congregation who have similar stories: those who think of their prodigal child while watching a baptism, who grieve their own spouses every time they read of a new marriage in the bulletin or who are so deep in debt that any mention of tithing makes them feel ashamed.

The danger is that if we do not know their stories, we have great potential to unknowingly wound them again—as I did with the mother. But, as nineteenth-century British pastor Joseph Parker wrote, "preach to the suffering and you will never lack a congregation. There is a broken heart in every pew."[1]

The better we know them, the better we can preach to them.

Learn the Culture

Every worshiping body has a culture. You may be able to close your eyes and picture exactly where people will sit, week after week. That's part of their culture. There may be a certain hymn always sung at Christmas, and always in Dutch. That's part of their culture. Funeral meals may always include thickly sliced ham on soft potato rolls spread with butter, or Navajo tacos, or cornbread. That's part of their culture.

When you are new to a congregation—or even when you are there as a guest preacher for one Sunday—you can stumble on aspects of culture they don't even realize are unique to them. In more formal environments, for example, you may run into some of these issues: people don't stand immediately when a song is announced but wait until the organist increases the volume on the last line of her played introduction. (Meanwhile, you pop up quickly and then awkwardly sit down.) Someone chimes the bells after the blessing but before the preacher is to walk down the aisle (as you remember when you are halfway to the back).

The Bible bearer will come up during the last verse of the hymn to remove the Bible from the pulpit (as you stand there belting out a hymn and suddenly have to move).

Or, in more informal environments, people will wander in and out to fetch coffee or get another cookie, or someone will come forward and kneel in front of church and pray aloud while you are speaking, or a child will come forward to select a banner from a basket and wave it wildly in the middle of the sermon—all of which can distract you from preaching.

Some of these things come from the ethnic culture, some are common in certain denominations and some are unique to that particular congregation. When we use these cultural markers in our preaching, it is a signal to the congregation that we are paying attention to the things they value. When you say about a funeral, "we were eating ham buns in the church basement," they notice.

One of the wisest things you can do is to know the history of your church better than anyone else. Some of us planted the congregations we are serving, so we know the history inside and out. Others walk past the black and white photos of somber, bearded men lining the main hallway and know a thick book about the church's centennial is available in the board room. In either case, weaving the history of the church into your preaching is a great way to show the people that they are not the only ones who have sat where they are sitting, that they are part of a long heritage of faith, and that getting to know the history of this place is important to you. Using their own shared story as an illustration or example in the sermon is a way to teach the story to those who do not know it, and to point out God's faithfulness to those who wonder about it.

Congregational or denominational culture is one thing, but some of us also preach in ethnic or national cultures foreign to our own. A colleague of mine who serves a church in an Asian country told me about a North American preacher who came for a visit. As part of his trip the preacher led worship for a large group of young adults. In his sermon the visiting preacher used an extended illustration about owning a car. My colleague said to me, "None of our young people ever dream of owning their own car. It's simply impossible for them." She told me that because the audience could not connect with that illustration, the rest of the sermon fell flat.

A better example is how Paul, a Jew from Tarsus, addressed the Greeks in Athens:

> Then Paul stood in front of the Areopagus and said, "Athenians, I see how extremely religious you are in every way. For as I went through the city and looked carefully at the objects of your worship, I found among them an altar with the inscription, 'To an unknown god.' What therefore you worship as unknown, this I proclaim to you." (Acts 17:22-23)

Paul honors the religious inclinations of the Greeks and also refers to their poets—the culture shapers of the day—when he says, "For 'in him we live and move and have our being'; as even some of your own poets have said, 'For we too are his offspring'" (Acts 17:28). Paul notices important parts of their culture, refers to them with respect and then builds on those ideas to teach them about resurrection. This is an excellent example of contextual and crosscultural preaching.

Gestures, idioms and cultural references often get us into trouble when we are attempting to preach to a culture not our own. If it's possible and if there is time, it would be wise to practice your sermon in front of someone from the culture you are preaching in, or at least have someone read the manuscript. If the person can be present for a practice, ask her or him to listen to your words and watch your body language. The person can even coach you on attire.

We also want to be as inclusive as possible if there are a variety of cultures and backgrounds present. Saying, "as all Lutherans know" or "as all First Church members know" may sound exclusive to any guests in the pews.

The goal is to demonstrate appreciation—and even affection—for the culture we are preaching in. Whether it's a mention of the 4-H kids at the county fair, the great pastrami on Third and Main or the word *lutefisk*, we are showing our people that what matters to them matters to us. When we do this, we not only honor the people who love that culture but we also maximize the potential for the gospel to be well-received.

LANGUAGE IS DYNAMIC AND ADAPTIVE

Preaching contextually as well as crossculturally is a challenge. Even a shared language does not guarantee a shared meaning, as anyone who has said "pants" in a sermon in England will attest. (*Trousers* is the word they use. *Pants* refers to underwear.) Following teenagers on social media will also make you aware of old words that have new meaning. Language is dynamic and adaptive.

Because of this we need to be aware of the language we use from the pulpit. Do you hear the word *admonition* in daily speech? Does the evening news anchor ever say "Thus"? Does the word *atonement* appear on social media? Even words that are common in religious speech may need translation as we present them to a contemporary audience. *Sin* can sound harsh when the only time we hear it is from the mouths of protestors. *Blessed* becomes cliché when everyone uses it as a hashtag.

We preachers are also notorious for using biz speak in our sermons. I once used the word *pericope* in a sermon and a college classmate of mine who was by then a college professor asked me afterward what it meant (the word refers to a short section of Scripture). I realized that if he didn't know what it meant, no one else in the congregation did either. *Hermeneutics, homiletics, eschatology, pneumatology* and even words like *kingdom, ethics* or *epistle* may need some translation. As I said before when talking about language for God, "using the 5 cent synonym right after the 25 cent term and doing this routinely week after week" is a way of caring well for our congregants and expanding their vocabulary of faith at the same time.[2]

One of the helpful features in many word-processing programs is that you can check readability statistics for anything you are writing. You can usually access this feature through the "Spelling & Grammar" tab. With a few clicks you can determine the grade level of the piece you're writing. PhD dissertations come in around grade 10. Sermons should come in around grades 5-7. Here again, if your current context is a university town with a congregation in which the vast majority of adults have advanced degrees, you may be able to pitch your language a bit higher. But remember that in most of our churches there are almost always children who quickly tune out if the language isn't at their level. The presence of children is also a reminder to keep sermons rated G, especially when speaking about sex or violence.

To preach contextually means preaching for the people who are before you, honoring their stories, their history, their culture and their language so nothing impedes the impact of the gospel.

How Did Jesus Preach?

Our best model for this (and everything else!) is Jesus. Jesus' parables are contextual. They are drawn from the daily lives of the people who were listening. Imagine Jesus smiling at the new bride and groom sitting on the hillside as he tells a story of a wedding banquet. Imagine him catching the eye of a finicky homemaker as he talks about a woman who loses a coin in her house. Imagine Jesus spotting the baker as he talks about yeast, or the angler as he speaks about fish, or the shepherd as he teaches about that one lost sheep.

Jesus knew his hearers—so well, in fact, that it sometimes alarmed them (e.g., to Nathanel: "I saw you under the fig tree" [Jn 1:48], and to the woman at the well: "You are right in saying, 'I have no husband'; for you have had five husbands, and the one you have now is not your husband" [Jn 4:17-18]). When Jesus preached, he preached about the lives of the people before him. Often the immediate issues of their lives prompted a parable, especially in the Gospel of Luke:

> But wanting to justify himself, [the lawyer] asked Jesus, "And who is my neighbor?" Jesus replied, "A man was going down from Jerusalem to Jericho, and fell into the hands of robbers." (Lk 10:29-30)

> "Teacher, tell my brother to divide the family inheritance with me." But [Jesus] said to him, "Friend, who set me to be a judge or arbitrator over you?" And he said to them, "Take care! Be on your guard against all kinds of greed; for one's life does not consist in the abundance of possessions." Then he told them a parable. (Lk 12:13-16)

> All the tax collectors and sinners were coming near to listen to him. And the Pharisees and the scribes were grumbling and saying, "This fellow welcomes sinners and eats with them."
> So he told them this parable. (Lk 15:1-3)

Jesus used the situations of the people around him to shape his preaching. Jesus preached big ideas in a way that connected with the daily lives of the people who were listening. The parables were for those people, on that day and in that place. In fact, Jesus' parables are so contextual to their time and place that we are still trying to unravel some of them. (How unusual was it for a father to run? How much power did judges have? What did it mean to lose one coin?)

Jesus was not a guru on a mountaintop, doling out proverbs. He was a teacher who told stories drawn from the daily lives of the people who were listening, and through these stories he sought to draw them to God.

Jesus preached big ideas in a way that connected with the daily lives of the people who were listening.

When we preach to our people on a particular day and in a particular place, hoping to draw them to God, we are imitating what Jesus himself did.

Pastoral Care from the Pulpit

The preacher of a growing congregation was approached by members of his board. They were paying attention to his time and wanted to help him steward his energy well. The strong preaching was certainly helping the church to grow, but as the church grew the preacher could no longer do all of the pastoral work required—visit the elderly, teach Sunday school, meet with new members, officiate all the weddings, preside over all the funerals. They suggested that he lay down the pastoral duties and simply focus on preaching.

The preacher listened to their well-reasoned opinions. He was grateful for their care for him. But he respectfully declined. "Preaching is part of the way I care for the people," he said. "If I don't know what is going on in their lives, I can't address it from the pulpit. The ministries of preaching and pastoral care go hand-in-hand." He used examples from recent sermons and pointed out that, unbeknownst to many in the congregation, certain examples, illustrations or applications were chosen specifically because of his pastoral care work. "The mention of porn or eating disorders isn't incidental—it's because I know members who are struggling with these things. The same with mentions of depression or grief or parenting. Every illustration I choose arises out of a relationship I have with someone in the congregation who will be touched by the mention—even if no one else knows."

His preaching was strong because it was contextual—it arose from the needs of the congregation, needs that he knew about because of the time he spent with them chatting in coffee shops, meeting around conference tables and praying at bedsides. This preacher read the Scripture text for the week as a pastor—as *their* pastor. His love for the congregation informed his research of the text. His hopes for them as a church fed his preaching. He knew that stepping out of pastoral care was not the best solution, and his church leaders quickly agreed. Together, they devised a new model of connecting with people that would not demand quite as much time but would still keep him in regular contact with parishioners: visiting elderly members every other month rather than every month with deacons filling in, finding a coteacher for the twelfth-grade church school class, letting the board run the new-member class. The leaders saw how important it was to keep preaching connected to pastoring.

Because preaching is the public face of our ministries and pastoral care is often behind the scenes, many parishioners do not know how often the conversations we have with members about faith, prayer, doubt, health, God, sex or death feed into our sermons. Preaching and pastoral care go hand in hand.

LOVE THEM, EVEN IF YOU DON'T LIKE THEM

If we're honest, sometimes we are tempted to let someone else visit everyone and listen to all of the problems so that we can hole up with our commentaries and novels and Greek New

Testaments and try to build sermons. It's even more tempting if things aren't going so well in your church.

It can be hard to preach a sermon for a particular context if you don't particularly like your context. If you're having disagreements with your board, people are arguing about worship styles or it seems that some people have it in for you, then it can be very hard to write sermons that care well for them. We all have parishioners whose names come across our emails or whose faces pop in the door and we feel an internal "ugh." The bossy elder. The gossipy deacon. The small-business owner who drives a luxury car but never gives. The member who sends you emails almost daily and complains if you don't respond immediately. The gruff old guy who greets you every Sunday with "Must be nice to only work one day a week."

You're thinking of someone right now, aren't you? The person who doesn't do anything worthy of church discipline but is simply annoying and hard to work with. And you know what we've all done: try to write a sermon for that person. The sermon on stewardship. The sermon on kindness. The sermon on "quick to listen, slow to speak." And on that day when we had that perfect sermon? The person wasn't there.

That's not contextual preaching. Contextual preaching is not writing a sermon with one person in mind (Take that, you selfish twit!). It is preaching with the whole church in mind. And it's putting our own agenda on the shelf and receiving the agenda God has for them. This is the hard, spiritual work of preaching.

In my context, preaching to college students, I want to tell them all the reasons why getting drunk every weekend or having casual sex outside of marriage is dangerous—physically, emotionally and spiritually. I want to rant against porn. I want to tell them to stop whining. I want to tell them how to dress and how to eat and to get more sleep. But none of that is the gospel. It's a revelation of my fear. I'm afraid of them becoming addicted to porn, getting pregnant or relying on caffeine to fuel a life of never saying no. I'm afraid for them. At its best, that fear leads me to rely on God's action in their lives. At its worst, it pushes me to preach sermons that sound bossy.

If our parishioners are really God's beloved children, and if the church is really the bride of Christ, then our job from the pulpit is not to bully anyone into better behavior. Our calling is not to save them. That job has already been taken. Our calling is to preach Christ and him crucified, and trust that the Holy Spirit will do the rest. Good contextual preaching demands that we love these people as Jesus loves these people, and trust God to take care of them.

> **Our job from the pulpit is not to bully anyone into better behavior. Our calling is to preach Christ and him crucified, and trust that the Holy Spirit will do the rest.**

EVALUATING CONTEXTUAL PREACHING

Those who teach preaching at Calvin Theological Seminary in Grand Rapids, Michigan, value contextual preaching to the point that it is one of the four categories they ask people to evaluate when their students go out to preach (the other categories are biblical, authentic and life changing).[3]

On the contextual section of the Sermon Evaluation Form, they write that "Preachers must demonstrate an awareness of the culture, the issues of the day, and the particulars of a given congregation (if the preacher is in a position to be familiar with the congregation). With this in mind, please evaluate this particular sermon."

The following are a few of the criteria from that part of the form:

1. The sermon made a connection between the biblical world and our current situation.

2. The sermon showed an awareness of contemporary issues.

3. The sermon was delivered in language that fits our contemporary world and that was therefore communicationally effective.

4. The sermon revealed God's active presence and grace in our world today and in the situations people face today.

Giving this form to your elders or board (or youth group, choir, etc.) will encourage you to preach sermons that minister to these people in this church on this day.

Put Them in the Story

Centuries ago Anglo-Saxon tribes had a scop (pronounced *shop*), who was the minstrel or bard of the tribe. One historian describes the role of the scop:

> The kings and nobles often attached to them a scop, or maker of verses. . . . The banquet was not complete without the songs of the scop. While the warriors ate the flesh of boar and deer and warmed their blood with horns of foaming ale, the scop, standing where the blaze from a pile of logs disclosed to him the grizzly features of the men, sang his most stirring songs, often accompanying them with the music of a rude harp.[4]

This is an ancient art form, of course, and we can see how even David served as a scop of sorts in the courts of King Saul. What was unique about the Anglo-Saxon scop, however, is that when warriors returned grieving the loss of those who had died that day, the scop would sing the story of the tribe from the very beginning. He would tell the story all of them had heard again and again, but when he finished all they had heard before he would add a verse. In the new verse would be the names of the fallen. Those names would be repeated again and again, as long as the song was sung. The names of the fallen were woven into the grand song of their people.

To preach in our contexts is to sing the song of our people; it is to put their names in the Story. This is the joy of preaching: taking the wounds and joys of our people, their losses and victories, and naming them in such a way that they can see how their stories are woven into the Story. That is the beauty and goal and pleasure of preaching. We are not clinicians; we are not tacticians. We are singers of the Song.

seven

Relevant Preaching

"I never know what I am supposed to do with what she says. It's interesting, and I learn a lot, but it's more like a Bible class than a sermon." Sarah sat across from her youth elder, cupping her tea mug with both hands. Sarah, thoughtful, reflective and smart, was a senior in the youth group.

"Like when she told us about Jewish wedding ceremonies when she preached on that parable about the bridesmaids? That was cool and really interesting, but I don't know how that's supposed to affect my life."

Brian, the youth elder, listened carefully. The elders and pastor had asked him to talk with some of the students about the preaching ministry of the church. Sarah was the third student he'd met with, and her words echoed the others'. There was genuine appreciation for the pastor and her sermons. The students loved her personality and how she obviously enjoyed teaching about biblical culture and customs, but each of them was unclear about the Bible's connection to their lives.

The good news? They really wanted that connection.

Most people do. They really want to know how the Bible affects their lives now. How should they live differently because of a sermon? What should its impact be? Bible knowledge is important, and historical information can be interesting, but the difference between a Bible class and a sermon is that while a Bible class can impact what we *know*, a sermon needs to also impact how we *live*.

The question that enlivens our preaching and moves us toward application is, *What does God do in our lives if this story is true?* How will God change our stories as we read and hear the Story? If God changed your congregation as a result of this sermon, what would they be doing?

Moving from the Abstract to the Practical

This is the heart of the challenge. How do we take something poetic or parabolic and make it practical? To help us, we'll walk through a familiar passage and then think about creative ways to apply that passage to the lives of our listeners. Drawing from chapter three on grace-full preaching, we also want to be clear that it is God's power that works in us. So we will be intentional about naming the work of the persons of the Trinity as we think about applying the sermon in the lives of our listeners.

We'll begin with the passage used in chapter four. The passage is from Matthew 5, the part of the Sermon on the Mount in which Jesus teaches his disciples to "let your light shine." Jesus' disciples did not then and cannot now literally shine, so we know that he is using a metaphor. But what is he talking about?

In a time without electricity, light was a precious commodity, and in the darkened landscape a small light could be seen from far away. For someone lost in the dark or trying to find his or her way home, a small light could be the difference between life and death. So Jesus' metaphor is about being seen, being visible and being known by others as someone who lives differently and illuminates dark places. It could even be said that "shining light" is about drawing people home.

If we are to move this idea from the metaphorical (Shine in dark places!) to the practical, a first step would be to name the dark places that exist today. Since we swim in artificial light and actually have to choose literal darkness, a more helpful question to ask may be, Where are the places of spiritual darkness? Where are the places in our lives where ugliness or disobedience or lies abound? Where are the places people struggle to have hope? For the members of your congregation, where are the dark places? Where are they are afraid? Where in our world does it seem that evil is winning?

It may be helpful to think about this by imagining the different ages and experiences within your church. Where is the darkness in families, on athletic teams, in business, in long-term care facilities or in schools?

Families often hide their darkness—the yelling, the anger, the contempt for each other. Athletic teams too often marginalize the weaker or younger players. Practices in business and industry can encourage people to get away with little things. Long-term care facilities can be places of deep loneliness. For many students school is where they learn what they aren't good at, who doesn't like them or that they will never make it.

How do we need Jesus' help to shine light in these places? Application is preached in the context of grace, so we don't want this to be all about us. God is at work in us, through us and with us to do the work of building his kingdom. Remembering this, you can now make a list of seemingly small ways your hearers can ask for God's help to shine light in these places.

Jesus can help you to

- commit as a family to new ways of speaking and listening to each other; maybe consider counseling

- ask an older teammate to stop picking on the freshmen

- tell the truth on all expense reports
- commit to pray for each grandchild every day, and tell them that you are praying
- volunteer to stay in for recess and tutor someone who is struggling

You can extend your imagination to also think about your city, county, state, nation or world. How can Jesus use us to shine against the darkness in these places? This list can include big things, grand ideas for how to influence our world.

Jesus can help us to

- participate in a cleanup event for a local park (you could do this as a church)
- join a mission enterprise to rebuild part of a country hit by disaster
- learn another language to work with refugees
- host homeless people in your church
- run for office
- go back to school

You can come up with many more ideas that have particular relevance for your community.

As you think about the application of your sermons, think about presenting the ideas as a bouquet of options. Not everyone is in school and not everyone can learn another language, so give ideas that are easier (commit to pray for each grandchild) as well as ideas that may stretch people (rebuild a war-torn country). Don't be afraid to offer really big ideas! Sometimes the Holy Spirit is looking to use our sermons to prod someone to make a significant life change. Sometimes being challenged to "sell all you have and give it to the poor" is exactly what someone needs to hear.

If we are honest with ourselves, there are times we pull back from a clear application because we don't think anyone will actually do what we are suggesting or, worse, we fear that we may actually need to practice what we've preached! Developing good application takes personal humility.

Developing good application takes personal humility.

We need to sit under the text and let it direct us before we can suggest its direction for anyone else. What God does with the text in our own lives isn't usually a part of the preached message, but we know that it is often part of the personal challenge of preaching: this text actually applies to me too.

Sometimes We Know, but Don't Want to Say It

Another challenge in the arena of application is when we know what the passage is asking of us and of our people, but we really don't want to say it.

Carlos was working through a series on 2 Corinthians and had arrived at chapter 9. When he had laid out the series, he knew this was coming. He knew he'd have to teach about money. He didn't want to. A few wealthy families footed the bills for most things in his church, allowing the majority of his congregants to skate along. When he'd asked the deacons for the list of donors and the amounts they gave, his concerns were confirmed. Twelve percent of his members gave weekly, ten percent gave monthly, and the rest gave occasionally. Christmas and Easter numbers were higher, but the overall picture was bleak.

Carlos hadn't preached on money in the three years he'd been at the church. He hadn't felt the need to. The budget was met every year, and a phone call or two would cover any additional expenses. But he knew that giving was not about meeting the budget. Giving was part of the Christian life. Even if the local congregation was swimming in cash, church members were still invited to give.

He could avoid the topic, deflect the sermon into the idea of "sowing and reaping," and use illustrations about people who were kind to others receiving kind actions in return. But that was karma, not gospel.

Carlos read the passage again: sowing, reaping, cheerful giving. Paul really lays it out there: part of a response to what God has done for us in Christ is to generously give back. Carlos had to preach on money. He had to invite his people to give.

Like Carlos, many of us squirm when we are faced with a troublesome text. For Carlos it was a passage about money. For others, texts about sexual ethics, care for the poor or support for government officials can give us pause. The truth is, any passage that moves us into a controversial area for our people (or our city, nation or world) is a tough one to preach.

It's hard to talk about money when it's the measure of success for so many. It's hard to talk about sex when what people do with their bodies is often framed in the language of choice and rights. It's hard to talk about caring for the poor or supporting government officials when people on either end of the political spectrum could hear the sermon as either going too far or not going far enough.

Sometimes we avoid applying a text because we don't have the energy to go three rounds with Cliff after worship. We don't want Angela mailing us pamphlets. We don't want links to videos sent to us in our email. We just don't want the fight.

Sometimes, though, the text won't let us off the hook. The passage is right there, and we need to say something about it. What are our options?

One less sanctified option is to blast people with the text, particularly if we have an agenda we'd like to advance (You must give more! It is a sin not to give regularly to the work of the church!). This often arises out of our own anger or frustration with our congregation and reveals more about us than it reveals about God. This also often leads to disputes among and bitterness within our hearers, so while we may have moments in our studies when we dream of yelling the application at people, these are moments best left out of the pulpit.

Another poor option is to preach the application so blandly that people miss it: "So God really loves a cheerful giver. Let's remember that as we go out this week." When we do this, we can think that we were faithful to the text and its application, but the truth is we intentionally avoided any pain for ourselves or any discomfort for the congregation. And sometimes applications are a bit uncomfortable.

When we are facing an application we do not want to offer, we first need to understand our own resistance. Is it because we aren't living the way God is inviting us to live? Is it because we don't want to be accused of preaching an agenda? Is it because we think people won't listen, that they will be angry or that they will leave? If we hope to name the truth for our listeners, we need to name the truth for ourselves.

This also helps us to have compassion for those who, like us, may find themselves resisting this application, and then moves us toward gentleness as opposed to either blasting anyone or obfuscating the truth.

When we spend time with the application and name our fears for how God may be using it in our own lives, we can then also celebrate the grace that God gives. *Every application of every text is a celebration of the grace of God that enables us to live differently.* We do

> **Every application of every text is a celebration of the grace of God that enables us to live differently.**

not give, change, obey or shine as a result of self-will or reso-
lution. We do so because God empowers us to do so.

One way to ensure this in our sermons is to use *God active*
language. Place God in the sentence as the agent who enlists our
help. For example, saying "God invites us to," "God empowers us
to" or "God helps us to" in the application section reminds us
that we live with God's help and in response to God's grace.

Every application flows out of the gospel—God has moved
toward us in Christ, God animates our lives by the power of
the Holy Spirit and we live in response to what God has already done.

When we are reluctant to preach an application, it may be
because we have missed the gospel that flows through it. Framing
any call to action as part and parcel of the gospel narrative allows
us to preach even hard applications as good news, because such
application is really our embodiment of the gospel itself.

For Carlos this may mean that the application part of his
sermon on 2 Corinthians 9 includes something like the following:

> It would be easy for us to read this section of Paul's letter
> and simply choose to be nice to each other. To live in such
> a way that we reap what we sow. But as we have seen, Paul's
> intent in chapter 9 was to call the Corinthians to give. To
> actually give their money to other people as a response to
> what God had done for them.
>
> Many preachers don't like to preach about money, and
> I'll admit it's not my favorite thing to do either. Preachers
> don't want to be seen as greedy, or only concerned about
> the budget, or insensitive to the financial challenges that
> some members have. But it would be vocationally irre-
> sponsible of me not to remind all of us that what we do
> with our money is a demonstration of our discipleship.

That's what Paul is saying. What we do with our money is a demonstration of our discipleship, which is why God loves a cheerful giver. And to make giving a regular part of our worship is one way we all demonstrate our discipleship together.

Maybe some of us have given on occasion, when we had a little extra. Maybe some of us give every week and it's part of our personal budget. Maybe some of us have never given. God is inviting us today to look at our giving to see if we are where he wants us to be. Not where the deacons would like us to be or where I would like us to be, but where God would like us to be. What is God inviting us to do?

Maybe giving something every week is what he is asking of you. Or setting up a personal budget that includes generosity to others. Maybe you'd like to meet with a deacon and learn more about tithing.

God loves you, and he loves our church, and he loves cheerful givers. God will lead you to respond cheerfully as he invites us all to give.

In this application Carlos admits his discomfort, offers clear suggestions, uses God active language and frames all of it as part of what it means to be a disciple.

God uses the texts we preach to change us—even when we don't want him to. To preach the application well is preaching the gospel itself: God converts people again and again, calling us from death to life.

How to Apply It: A Case Study
from the Book of James

Many sources are ready to tell us what the Bible really says about the end times, sex, money or hell. From little booklets at grocery store checkout lines to some cable TV preachers, many people are eager to tell us that finding out what the Bible says about something and then doing it is pretty easy.

But those of us who engage the book professionally (as well as personally) know that interpreting Scripture is much more complicated than listing a few proof texts on the topic of the day. We work to find out the author's intent, the original audience, the historical context and the subtleties of language to discern what the author may have meant when the text was first written. But even when we know what the text says and what it meant in its context (e.g., "don't eat meat offered to idols" or "you shall be holy, as I am holy"), it can be hard to know what that application should look like in our context.

To illustrate this challenge, I am going to use the case study of a tough passage from the book of James. We'll read it, study it and imagine possible ways to apply it. We'll use it as an example of applying a passage to the lives of our hearers.

Initial reading. The passage from James is a diatribe against the rich.

> Come now, you rich people, weep and wail for the miseries that are coming to you. Your riches have rotted, and your clothes are moth-eaten. Your gold and silver have rusted, and their rust will be evidence against you, and it will eat your flesh like fire. You have laid up treasure for the last days. Listen! The wages of the laborers who mowed your fields, which you kept back by fraud, cry out, and the cries of the harvesters have reached the ears of the Lord of hosts. You have lived on the earth in luxury and in pleasure; you have fattened your hearts in a day of slaughter. You have condemned and murdered the righteous one, who does not resist you. (Jas 5:1-6)

This strong passage has many ideas woven throughout. At first glance we may come up with a few potential applications of this text:

- Rich people are innately evil, and therefore all of us should avoid accumulating wealth.

- We shouldn't have retirement funds and should trust God alone.

- Those of us who employ others, are supervisors or oversee people in any way need to pay them fairly and treat them well.

- Those of us who purchase goods and services should do what we can to ensure that we are not supporting business or industry that exploits people.

It could be said that this passage from James is a *shotgun text* as opposed to a *rifle shot text*. A shotgun fires a shell that contains many small ball bearings or BBs. When the shell is fired, the ball bearings spread across the target, increasing the chances that something will be hit. Firing a shell that contains many ball bearings allows a hunter to hit the target even if the aim isn't perfect. A rifle, on the other hand, fires a single bullet in the hopes of hitting the target in one shot.

Some texts are like a rifle shot: there is a single, clear way to apply them. Many texts are shotguns shells: there may be a number of ways they can hit a target.

In this passage from James we can imagine the application could be any of those listed earlier. But we want to get as close to the target as possible. So we read commentaries and study the Greek text to determine what may be at the heart of James's concerns.

Going deeper. Scholars tell us that in this section of his letter James is writing about nonbelieving rich farmers who aren't actually going to read what he's written.[1] In the section just before this he is writing to Jewish Christians who were being seduced by the idea that they could plan their lives in such a way as to make money: "Today or tomorrow we will go to such and such a town and spend a year there, doing business and making money" (Jas 4:13). In the section after this one James is most likely addressing the poorer members of the communities he is writing to, encouraging them to be patient because "the coming of the Lord is near" (Jas 5:8).

So what is the purpose of this rant against the rich? We find that while James would indeed want his readers to treat laborers well, and while he would indeed want them to support people who did just that, the core of his concern is that the readers he is addressing in James 4:13-17 will become like the unbelieving rich he takes on in James 5:1-6. Woven into his diatribe are references to the Sermon on the Mount, where in Matthew 6:19-21 Jesus warns his disciples that earthly treasures can be stolen or consumed, so his disciples are invited to store up their treasures in heaven. There is also a subtle nod to the parable told in Luke 12, where Jesus reminds his hearers to be on their guard against all kinds of greed, and then tells them the story of a rich man who tore down small barns to build bigger barns and was then scolded by God: "'You fool! This very night your life is being demanded of you. And the things you have prepared, whose will they be?' So it is with those who store up treasures for themselves but are not rich toward God" (Lk 12:20-21).

James doesn't want these disciples to envy the rich. He doesn't want them to have it as their goal in life to "do business and make money." So he paints a stark picture of what happens to people who make accumulation their chief goal: their goods will rust away and the evidence of that "will eat your flesh like fire."

What is God up to? The chief concern of James is that his dear people are starting to envy the rich, and this could lead them down a dangerous road. James wants his readers to remember that God has promised to care for whatever they need, and envy is a turn away from trusting God.

If the chief concern of James is the envy of the rich, and his primary hope is that his readers will turn away from envy to trust in God, then what applications may there be for us and for our congregations?

To get to the application, we may be helped by asking and answering a series of questions.

1. Why do we envy the rich?

2. What things do we see that increase this envy?

3. What is the opposite of envy?

4. What practices does God call us to (as individuals, families, households, a church) that will move us away from envy and toward contentment?

The following are possible answers.

1. Why do we envy the rich? We envy the rich because it appears their lives are easier than ours. They have nothing to worry about because all of their needs are met. They can buy what they want when they want it, while we budget and tithe and barely get by. Plus, they have nicer things: softer clothes and better shoes and appliances that work, and cars with heated seats and surround-sound stereos. Our lives, we are convinced, would be better if we were rich.

2. What things do we see that increase this envy? Movies we watch take place in swanky New York apartments. We see television shows set on palatial English estates. The Sunday paper is packed with ads. Catalogs clog our mailboxes, and we look at the shiny pictures of pretty people wearing tweed and walking their dogs and think, *I want a different life!*

3. What is the opposite of envy? Envying the wealth of others makes us deeply discontented with what we have. Our clothes are out of style and the seats of our cars are cold. What's the opposite of envy? Contentment. As a plaque in my mother's kitchen says, "Contentment is not the fulfillment of what we want, but the realization of how much we already have." Envy kills contentment.

4. What practices does God call us to (as individuals, families, households, a church) that will move us away from envy and toward contentment?

    1. God may be calling us to filter what we let in.

        a. We can recycle the Sunday paper inserts and the catalogs before we even look at them.

        b. We can review our screen time and ask if what we are watching is creating envy or contentment.

    2. God may be calling us to practice gratitude.

        a. Encourage people to start a gratitude list. Every night before sleep, list five specific things you are thankful for from that day.

        b. If members share meals with others (roommates, family, friends), they could name the five things together when they eat.

        c. As a church, you could start a gratitude wall (or blog), thanking God for what you see happening at church.

        d. You could write letters to the local paper, naming members of your community you are thankful for.

        e. You could write to store owners and store headquarters, thanking them for great service or for business practices that you appreciate.

3. God may be calling us to serve others.

    a. What if the church youth groups had an opportunity to serve each month, instead of doing one big trip each year?

    b. What is one need in your church's neighborhood that the church could start to meet, so that in a year or two things would be different for a local family, apartment complex, school or business?

    c. Is there a local agency that is already providing clothes, food or health care for people that could be a great long-term partner for your congregation?

4. God may be calling us to advocate for others.

    a. Some companies, for example, are open Thanksgiving Day, no longer allowing their employees to enjoy the holiday. Some companies may employ workers in other countries at subsistence wages. Some companies may not practice careful workplace safety. How do we now view spending or not spending our money at these stores in light of James 5?

    b. If there are business owners in our congregations, are we giving them every help so they can offer good wage and benefit packages to their employees? Are we expecting this of ourselves and those we worship with?

    c. Are we praying for God's blessing on the business people who are acting with integrity?

5. God may be calling us to give.

    a. How much money does your church give away? Do your members know how much of their money given to the church goes toward local and global poverty-fighting efforts? Do they hear stories of people who have been impacted by the church's generosity?

b. Many local agencies receive most of their donations (food, money, clothing) at the end of the year. Maybe your church can learn when they are most in need (spring?) and organize giving to coincide with times of deepest need.

6. God may be calling us to confess sin and receive pardon.

a. Many of us have plenty, and we are not always very grateful. Many of us buy what we want, where we want and ignore the practices that brought the goods and services to us. Many of us have "laid up treasures for the last days" just as the rich farmers named in James did. A key part of a sermon on wealth is to name that truth that many of us are wealthy (especially when compared with global levels of income).

b. Preaching guilt and shame about our wealth or about how we spend it will not animate our congregation or ourselves to action. But allowing us to confess the fact that we envy, that we are not content or that we are not generous will actually allow grace to enter in!

The main point of this passage is that God does not want us bound by wealth. He wants us to be free so he can show us how deeply he cares for us and will provide all that we need. Our God longs to "give us this day our daily bread." Moving away from envy and toward contentment is a way to move closer to God. The application is how we demonstrate ways we can partner with God in his kingdom work.

Love Them Through the Sermon

As you can see, this passage from James allows for many possible applications. How do you choose? Think about how to love your congregation through the sermon. Which application will have the most resonance for your congregation? Where are they most tempted to envy? What would excite them most: gratitude, serving, giving? How could you and your worship planners create a time of confession and forgiveness that gives God room to set people free? Here is where knowing your context can bear much fruit.

> **Think about how to love your congregation through the sermon.**

You know your people and what they need. Pray for them, and as you think about how to apply any passage, listen to the Spirit. He desires for your people to love the Word and to live it out.

The reason we work so hard at application is because we believe that Scripture is true. We believe that it reveals God at work in his world. And we believe that God wants us to join him in that work.

This is why preaching matters: it can actually change us. It can change our congregations, our cities and the world. When God gets to work on us, he can accomplish amazing things.

eight

Embodied Preaching

We all remember a teacher from our past who droned on, unaware of the note passing or napping happening around the class. We remember how the teacher was imitated in locker rooms or on the school bus. We can easily recall the snickering that happened when a teacher's pants were too short or her lipstick was smudged or her slip showed under her skirt. Some of us can still imitate the famed gesture of a seventh-grade civics teacher who always played with his tie or the art teacher who twirled her glasses.

All of the things we did to our teachers, our listeners do to us. I am sure that if you gather a group of the students I regularly preach to, they could spoof my delivery, my outfits and my gestures.

All of these things—vocal tone, appearance, gestures—fall under the category of sermon delivery.

It's tempting to think that these things don't matter, that the gospel is what matters and people should get over superficial things such as what we wear when we preach.

OUR BODIES MATTER

But here is the theological truth: the act of incarnation is at the core of the gospel. God took on flesh, became embodied. Jesus used his body to speak, teach, heal, walk, eat, embrace, listen, sleep, die and rise. We believe in a God who cares about what we do with our bodies. Our bodies matter to God.

Our bodies (voices, gestures) are tools for our preaching. God has called us to preach, and preaching is an embodied art, so we are responsible to use our bodies well when we preach. Paying attention to how our bodies help or hinder as we preach the gospel is significant for our ministries.

So here is the challenge: watch a video of yourself preaching. I know. It's painful. It's painful because we all have an idea of what we look like when we preach: we are taller, thinner and better looking. Our hands aren't glued to our sides. Our voices sound like James Earl Jones or Emma Thompson. Our makeup is perfect. Our shoes are shined. Our hair isn't as gray (or there is more of it!). Then we watch the video and we face the reality of potbellies, nervous gestures, the dress that is not very flattering, and *do I really sound like that?*

Part of the problem is this: who do we usually watch on-screen? Beautiful people. What do we see when we watch ourselves? Not-so-beautiful people. Let's face it, God did not call most of us to a modeling career for good reason. I think we can own that truth about ourselves. But before we get discouraged because the diet isn't working or we can't figure out what to do with our hands, remember that the goal of all of this is to communicate the gospel. This isn't a beauty pageant. This is church.

But there are still people who watch us—carefully—for at least an hour each week. If they have to do it, we have to do it.

So we'll watch the video and take notes. The following guide will help you know what to look for. As you go through this chapter, it may be helpful to select one bullet point from each section to work on, rather than try to improve all areas at the same time.

Using Your Body

The first time you watch a recorded sermon, watch with the sound off. As you watch the video, look at how you are using your body. This will allow you to focus on your incarnational pulpit presence. Get out a pen and pad (or stylus and tablet) and jot down what you notice.

Here are a few things to look for:

- Do you repeat certain gestures? Common ones involve glasses (adjusting them as they slide or taking them off and putting them on), holding one side of the pulpit more than the other, picking up something (Bible, notes) and then putting it down, taking a drink of water at certain points in the sermon, raising and then lowering the stand that your notes are on, or touching a part of your face (ears, nose, chin).

- Do you use one side of your body more than the other? This is particularly applicable if you hold something in one hand, such as your Bible or your notes. This means that one half of your body is engaged in holding something and is not free to be used as a tool for the sermon. We all also tend to use our dominant hand to gesture more.

- If you do not stay behind the pulpit, do you gravitate toward one area of the stage, chancel or platform? Do you know why you go there? We'll look at the physical space later in the chapter, but look at lighting, microphone cords, flowers and other obstacles that may limit your movement.

- Pay attention to where you are looking: do your eyes connect with every zone in the sanctuary—front third, middle third, rear third; right side, left side, balcony?

It's odd, but often the front rows get very little eye contact. Most of us also tend to look at one side more than the other.

- How do you move your head? Do you hold it in unnatural ways? We are thinking people and we like ideas. But this means we can strike postures that are more contemplative (for example, head to the side as if you are evaluating the truth of what you are saying) than declarative (head squared on shoulders, chin up slightly).

- If you hold a Bible while preaching, are you using it? If there is a Bible in your hand, give it purpose! Read from it or set it down open in a place where people can see it. Avoid closing it and sliding it back under the pulpit, as if you are saying, "Well, done with that. Now here's what I have to say!" Also avoid holding it the whole time you are preaching without referring to it.

- If you preach from a manuscript, how often and for how long do you look at it? We often underestimate how long our eyes are down. For those of us who appreciate the precise language of a written manuscript, then at minimum we can try to memorize the introduction, stories or illustrations, and the conclusion. Our listeners need to connect with us at those points in the sermon, and that happens through eye contact. If you watch a video of yourself and find that you see the top of your head because your eyes are down most of the time, practice reading your manuscript out loud at least three times before preaching it.

Each time you read it, the sermon is becoming more internalized and it will be much easier to keep your eyes up when you preach. Challenge yourself to look down only once per page. Consider also elevating the manuscript by

> raising the stand it sits on so you needn't dip your head so far down.

- When you look up from your notes or manuscript, do you do it in the same way every time? For example, you always lift your head and look to the right side, or you always glance left and take a breath before you slide one page over. At this point in the sermon, our thoughts are focused on what we are saying next, not on what our bodies are doing. A routine at this moment isn't a bad thing unless it is distracting to those who are listening.

And here's the big question: If the students in your youth group were going to imitate you, what would they do?

If you've done the hard work of watching yourself, well done. You probably have noticed a few things that need tweaking. (And if you haven't, ask a trusted member of the youth group or one of the children in your life to point out a few things.) Remember to start small rather than trying to change everything at once. Choose one item to improve and go from there.

Gestures Need Purpose

As we use our bodies, we want to do so in a way that enhances our preaching. Think about it this way: gestures need purpose. If we are lifting our arms, we should do so because we are describing something lofty or grand. If we fold our hands in front of us, it should be because that moment in the sermon is more calm. (And occasionally our bodies may reveal that an area of the sermon isn't as clear as it could be. If you find yourself making a circle gesture with your hand, as you may see when someone is telling you to just get on with it, it may signal that your brain is telling you to just get on with it and make the point.) We want our gestures to aid our preaching.

If the sermon is juxtaposing two ideas (Israel-Egypt; law-grace; faith-works) maybe the left side of your body is used for one (Israel) and the right side for the other (Egypt). You can use certain gestures to mark certain points: welcoming in, pushing away, turning aside, one hand up and the other down (like scales in the balance), folding your arms over your chest to indicate resistance, opening your arms and letting them drop to signal acceptance, or tapping the points of your sermon on your first, second and third fingers as you move through the sermon (though this has a high potential to be annoying, so monitor how often you use it).

As we use our bodies, we want to do so in a way that enhances our preaching.

Also be aware of how you can communicate a timeline with your body. When people are watching us, their timelines go from our right to our left. This feels backwards to us as we preach, but if we flip our gestures and put, say, the creation event at our far right and the return of Jesus at our far left, that will make perfect sense to those who are watching us. The same with Abraham (right), Isaac (center) and Jacob (left).

You can also mark out areas of the stage, chancel or platform for different times, places or people. Maybe one area is Paul and the other is the Philippians who are receiving his letter. Maybe one area is death and one is life. Then every time you move to that area, your parishioners have a tip as to which item you're going to be addressing. It's important that once you have committed to a gesture meaning a certain thing, it means that thing throughout the sermon. Don't change it up on the fly. It is very confusing to our people if the first time a gesture means death and the next time it means the apostle James.

Gestures and movements can not only be engaging for the congregation but also help us remember what we are saying! For those of us who preach without notes, kinesthetic memory can be an important part of internalizing the sermon. Your body helps you to remember that when you move in a particular way, you need to say a particular thing. This assumes that you'll practice the sermon a few times before you preach it, intentionally incorporating gestures that help you communicate.

For those of us who use manuscripts, and for all of us who read Scripture aloud in public, you may want to try something I call "snatch and speak." When we train worship leaders at our college, we have them stand up and read Scripture by looking down, memorizing a short phrase (snatching it) and saying the phrase all the way to the end while looking at the others in the room (speaking). If the student's eyes drop before she ends the sentence, we stop her and have her do it again. It sounds so easy, but invariably a student's eyes will drop to the next phrase before the first one is out of her mouth. Practicing snatch and speak inserts a slower pace into reading Scripture (or into preaching a manuscript). It also allows the speaker to focus on what she is saying in that moment before she moves on to the next line. It's easier with poems and prophecy than a narrative or an epistle, but it makes reading Scripture more of a communal event because the speaker is working to make eye contact with the hearers.

This is also why those of us who write manuscripts need to avoid sentences longer than twelve words; they are simply too hard to deliver well. This is the difference between writing for the eye and writing for the ear.[1] It is much easier to deliver shorter sentences.

The Sound of Your Voice

If you've watched a recording of yourself with the sound off, watch again with the sound on or listen to an audio recording.

Pay attention to the sound of your voice.

Here are some things to observe:

- What is the speed of your speaking? Many of us preach just a bit faster than our normal conversational pace, and sometimes this speed makes our words slur together. Conversely, there are some preachers who develop what is known as a "preaching voice": sonorous, slow and sliding from one pitch down an octave to another. It's the voice you hear when someone on television is mocking preaching. Let's try to avoid that.

- Does the speed match the space, the formality of the service and the language skills of the listeners? If you worship in a highly liturgical context with a printed liturgy, responsive readings, organ and robed choir, and the space is a tall steeple church in which everything has a slight echo, a slower pace may be needed. A slower pace may also be needed if you preach in a gym, stadium or outdoor amphitheater on a windy day. You may also need to slow down if you serve members who are not native speakers of the language you're preaching in. If you are blessed with excellent acoustics or a state-of-the-art sound system and the space is wired to help those with hearing loss, you may be able to speed up now and then.

- Does the speed vary throughout the sermon? If we think of a speed range from 1 to 10, with 1 being boringly slow and 10 being I-can't-understand-you fast, we can strive for a range from 4-6, with occasional dips to 3 and rises to 8. The danger is when everything is 6-7, 9-10 or, gulp, 1-2. If you have been preaching at a pretty good clip, slowing down significantly as you change points or move to application can be very effective. Don't make it a habit, though, because soon you will train your listeners that when you're speaking fast they don't need to pay attention, or that when you speak slowly you're almost done with the sermon.

- Does your volume rise and fall? I was speaking with a parishioner who loves his preacher, but he said to me, "Everything comes out loud and energetic. The whole sermon. Every sermon. It was fun to listen to at first, but honestly, it gets exhausting." And we may all have had the senior member of the congregation note that she misses some of what we say because our voices get too quiet, especially at poignant moments. Working on vocal variety allows you to give your listeners a break and helps you avoid saying everything meaningful too softly.

- When you say something exciting, sad or troubling, does your voice match it? If someone who doesn't know the language you are preaching in were to listen to you, could that person tell by your inflection the emotion or meaning you were trying to convey?

- Are there any words you don't pronounce well, or can you hear any vocal impediments such as a lisp, slurring of words or running words together? Granted, some of those biblical names and places are hard to pronounce, but do you notice extra *s* sounds at the ends of words? Do you say "Apostles' Creed" as "Apostles' Screed"?

- Does your volume drop at the end of sentences? This is a common problem, especially for those of us who preach from manuscripts. When our eyes drop to get to the next line, our voice often drops too. This is also a classic "preacher's voice" issue, when the volume and tone drop at the end of phrases.

- If you were an elderly member of the congregation, would some parts be too quiet to hear? Turn the volume down to the point at which you can just make out most of your words. What words can't you hear? Is there a section in the sermon that goes missing?

- If you were a younger member of the congregation, would any section of the sermon lack vocal variety? Would you remind them of the droning teacher? Either all loud and fast or all slow and low is too much of a good thing. Alter your cadence, pitch and volume to keep all ages interested. A conversational tone is a great default setting for most preachers, with room to go up or down as needed. Always loud and energetic makes every point sound equally important. Always reserved and calm may mean that nothing really matters.

- Care well for your voice. While it's tempting to yell at a game on Saturday night, this could mean that your voice is compromised for Sunday morning. Eating or drinking certain things before we speak may actually harm our vocal abilities. For example, eating a strong mint before you preach may actually dry out your mouth and make you cough. Dairy is known to cause excess phlegm for some people, so consider avoiding it before you preach. I once heard an opera singer suggest the idea of a sports drink before a performance (though she warned about avoiding bright colors as they coat the tongue!). In general, you want to stay hydrated and avoid the overuse of your voice before you preach.

A great resource for those of us who would like to improve our technical speaking abilities is *Getting the Word Across: Speech Communication for Pastors and Lay Leaders* by Robert

Jacks.[2] The book contains vocal exercises that are easy to do and can quickly help us to speak more clearly and dynamically.

I was once teaching a student who was a very bright, capable writer of sermons but struggled to deliver them. As she stood before the handful of others in her class, I had her try a section of her sermon one more time, and told her to pretend she was a preacher. She laughed, but as she began she was louder where she needed to be and quieter in the tender spots. She played with the rhythm of her words and the sermon came alive. When she was done, her classmates all sat up and applauded. She needed a little push to move from the excellent biblical scholar that she was to become the preacher she was meant to be. Did it feel normal to her? Not immediately. But will it improve her preaching? Yes.

You may find that your preaching voice is different from your everyday voice. Vocally speaking, preaching is a performance. It demands something different from us. Don't fake it; don't put on another voice. Be yourself, but as with my student, when you're up in front, you may need to be a bigger version of yourself.

Dress to Represent

It may be easy to dismiss thinking about what we wear when we preach; after all, few people come to their preachers for fashion tips. But the reality is that those who watch us preach pay attention to what we wear. What we wear depends on cultural expectations, the formality or informality of the worship experience, and personal style. With all of those things taken into account, our chief goal is to minimize anything that may be a distraction from the gospel message.

Here are a few tips:

- Dress one step up from your audience. If they are in shorts, wear pants. If they are in jeans, wear chinos. If they are in chinos, perhaps wear a skirt. If they are in ties, you're in a tie and jacket or a pantsuit. You get the idea. And if you are invited to preach in an unknown context, ask about appropriate attire. In some contexts the preacher is never seen not wearing a suit. In others it would be strange if the preacher didn't dress in jeans like everyone else. When in doubt, dress one step up.

- Wear conservative jewelry and no earrings that dangle. Dangling earrings are a sound technician's nightmare. If you are wearing a headset mic of any kind, the odds of an earring banging against it are high. Dangling earrings also can be visually distracting for your audience. The same goes for bracelets, watches or sparkly rings.

- If you think it may be too tight or revealing, don't wear it. Skirts, dresses and shorts should hit the knees. Even if you have great legs, we don't need to see them when you are preaching on the holiness codes in Leviticus. And please—do I have to say this?—no cleavage. None. Zero. Generally, nothing sleeveless either. No tight clothing means no yoga pants, skinny jeans or anything that draws the attention to your body and away from worship. Err on the side of a little more fabric all around.

- Empty your pockets. If we can see what kind of phone you have by looking at your front pocket, we may also wonder if you've remembered to turn it off. Why would you need your phone when preaching anyway? Emptying our pockets also gets rid of any keys and coins and limits any extraneous noise caused by their jingling. Pants lay better and look better when the pockets are empty.

- If your bangs fall in your face while you are speaking, get them trimmed or wear a clip. There are few things more annoying than a preacher who has to manage his or her hair while preaching.

• Dark pants are more flattering. On everyone. They also don't show the drops of tea that splashed on them when you pulled out the teabag in your car on the way to church. Light khaki pants rarely look good when you are standing in front of people. Go with navy or black pants, or darker jeans if the event is more casual.

• Solid colors are more flattering on top. You may want to avoid stripes, plaids or busy floral patterns for your shirts. Not only are solid colors more flattering on most people, but if your services are video recorded or livestreamed, solid colors work better, especially at slower download speeds. A patterned shirt can look like a test pattern when viewed online.

• If you are wearing a belt and shoes and people can see both, they should match. A brown belt requires brown shoes. A black belt, black shoes. Some of us have the fashion sense to wear a colored belt with dark shoes or something of the sort. If that's you: well done.

• Remember the microphone pack and cord have to go somewhere. A sheath dress looks great on many body types, but there is no place to hook on the battery pack for your microphone. The same is true with some of the long shirts or tunics favored by some cultures. You'll need to access a waistband. It's also distracting if we have a microphone cord falling off of our shoulders or moving around on the front of our shirts. Depending on the microphone, drop the cord down the back of your shirt and connect it with the waist pack there. In general, hide the cord and minimize its distraction to both you and the audience.

- If your context is more formal, wear traditional liturgical clothing (alb, suplice, cassock). Wearing a robe removes much of the anxiety associated with the items listed previously. You can wear the same pants, shoes, earrings or belt every Sunday and no one knows. I must say I love occasions when I can preach in my robe because it's one less thing to worry about as I prepare to preach.

SPACE IS IMPORTANT

If you've gone through the pain of watching yourself on video, you may want to watch it again. This time, take a good look at the sanctuary, auditorium or chapel and ask, Does this space help me preach?

- Do you have room to move? If you are not a walk-around preacher, do you at least have room to move your arms? If you like to have space to move more freely, do you have it? Be aware of the things that can clutter a pulpit: big pulpit Bibles, hymnals, bulletins. Is there anything you could knock over? Anything that looks like it will fall off?

- Does the size of the pulpit fit you? Could it be raised or lowered? Many preachers are taller than I am, and when I serve as a guest preacher in some churches, the pulpit is simply too big. When I preach in a large pulpit, I take on the appearance of a third grader. That's not really the look I'm going for. Some pulpits have adjustable stands, and in other places, yes, I've stood on a stool.

- Are you always stepping over cords or trying not to knock over microphone stands? With more people involved in worship leadership, the equipment of your average worship band can scatter all across the pulpit area. Is it distracting to you? If it is, it's distracting to those listening to you.

- What draws the eye—the band equipment, the organ, the choir, or the space (pulpit, stage) where the preaching happens? Sightlines are important, and it's best if they bring people's focus to where you are preaching. If the band leader is in front and the band's equipment is as well, you'll look like you're just filling in for the band while they take a break.

- Is there a large floral display that blocks your eye contact with part of the room or prevents movement? Plants can soften a space or hide monitors, microphones and cords. Use them strategically to create a great space for preaching. If they are misplaced, however, they can impede your connection with the audience.

- If there are windows above or behind you, how distracting are they? I know of a church in Colorado with clear glass behind the pulpit that reveals a stunning view of the mountains. While you wouldn't want curtains, you could darken the glass a shade so the image of the mountains remains but the congregation is less prone to daydream about skiing.

- If banners are hung, do they serve the preaching or distract from it? Are the banners excessively large, making the preacher look small? Do they draw the eye to the ceiling or keep it focused front and center?

We all know that dealing with the physical space of a church can be a challenge. We can run into problems because Mr. Rodriguez donated the pulpit, the women's guild made the banners, the band already feels second-class without having to move farther back on the platform, Mrs. Nordling arranges the flowers every week, and it would take a lot of money to remodel the choir loft, which is now directly behind you as you preach, allowing the choir members to note the gradual increase in the size of your bald spot.

Knowing all this, ask yourself, *If I could change one thing about the space, what would I change and why?* Perhaps showing your preaching video to a small group (elders? banner committee? worship leader?) and asking for their suggestions would help. While adapting the physical space may not stop people from noticing your receding hair line, it could decrease the number of visual distractions you have to battle while you preach.

PRACTICE, PRACTICE, PRACTICE

I recently took in a theater performance in which the stage was a pool of water surrounded by a deck. Actors would go in and out of the pool regularly, leaving the deck wet and slick. As they moved around the set, it became very apparent that they had rehearsed how to walk on a slippery deck. They had also practiced how to magnify their gestures so that they could be seen even when they were in the pool. They had planned what to do if they fell. It was obvious that their director had put them through their paces again and again so that when the time came, they were ready.

> In order to present the sermon in the best way possible, we need to practice.

Preaching is a type of performance, and we want to be ready. We want our bodies and our voices to work together. We want our gestures to aid and not distract. In order to present the sermon in the best way possible, we need to practice.

One way to use your practice time is to preach the sermon out loud three times before the worship service. For the first time through, consider sitting at a table with pen in hand. Read aloud and notice where you want to speed up and where you want to slow down. Find sentences longer than twelve words and split them up. Mark where you want to pause. You may find that reading the sermon aloud reveals some lack of clarity here and there; our brains process things differently when we hear them. Do the editing you need to do to make the sermon as clear as possible.

For the second time through, stand up. If you're in the church building, go into the sanctuary. If you're at home, find a make-shift pulpit. Place the manuscript or notes on the pulpit and preach the sermon through, using your edited notes from the first practice session. You may want to time your sermon to see if it is falling into your allotted range.

- *Body.* This time, as you preach, add gestures. What will help you tell the stories? Should you move from the right side of the stage to the left? Do you find that you're grabbing the pulpit with two hands for much of the sermon?

- *Eyes.* Can you easily tell any story in the sermon without looking down? Are you looking at all areas of the room, including in the areas right in front of you?

- *Voice.* Where do you need to slow down? Where do you need to pause? Is there good vocal variety? Use your everyday conversational voice from time to time, as if you are saying the words to a friend who is sitting in the room. If you were to chart your speed, would it be in the 4-6 range? What about volume?

The third time through try to preach more slowly than you think you should. Because you now know the sermon well, the temptation is to breeze through it. Instead, slow it down. Take a good breath every time you've marked a pause. Confirm that each gesture is communicating what you want it to. By this time you should be able to offer the introduction, any stories and the conclusion without looking down. Review the things from the second time through and continue to tweak your delivery.

If you want to preach without notes, practice it at least two more times without using the notes. The goal when preaching without notes is not to memorize a manuscript word for word but to internalize the structure of the message—its introduction, movements, points, stories and conclusion—so well that the message is coming as much from your heart as from your head.

Preaching from a manuscript allows a preacher to craft each word, and that may be enough of a value to you and your congregation that you do not want to give it up by attempting to preach without notes. Those who preach without notes appreciate the immediate connections that are made with their hearers. Because those who preach without notes are always looking at their listeners, they can see if they need to slow down or repeat a point. They can observe when people laugh or are particularly quiet, and adjust their delivery in the moment.

> The goal when preaching without notes is not to memorize a manuscript word for word but to internalize the structure of the message so well that the message is coming as much from your heart as from your head.

Preaching without notes takes more preparation, but for some of our contexts the gains made through the constant connection with our listeners are worth the extra time.

A FINAL WORD: BRING IN THE CLOWNS AND THE PROFESSORS

I love to watch standup comedians. I learn so much about cadence, timing and storytelling from them. I especially prefer those who are clean, not only because that aligns with my values but also because comedians who work clean cannot rely on the easy laughs that come with punctuating a routine with curses.

And since we can't cuss in the pulpit, we can learn the most from those who tell funny stories without so much as a "gosh." Do a Web search for "clean comics" and watch a few videos. Your colleagues may hear you laughing in the office, but you can legitimately tell them that you are working to improve your preaching. And after studiously watching yourself, you deserve a laugh.

You may also decide that it's time to have a communications professional sit down and watch one of your sermons. I suggest asking around for a college communications professor or the best speech teacher at a local high school. Send them a message and offer to pay for a few hours of their time for them to watch a sermon (or two) and give you some direct feedback. Ask the person for three specific ways you can improve. If they are amenable to the idea, ask them to make a commitment to return in three months for another review. It can be painful, but if in twelve months you are preaching better than ever, it will have been worth the pain.

Preaching is worthy of our best efforts. Spending time watching ourselves on video and honing our delivery is not done in order to look good but to minimize distractions and maximize the gospel. We are ambassadors of One who is greater than ourselves. We are heralds of God Almighty.

nine

Self-less Preaching

Five guys were standing together after church, coffee cups in hand. They were chuckling about the funny story the preacher had told about himself that morning. It was another in a series of stories that exhibited his inability to fix things.

"Aw, I get it. I'm the same way. If it involves something more than a hammer or a screwdriver, I'm worthless," said one of them. The men laughed. Others chimed in about home repair gone amok or the job that was supposed to take thirty minutes but swallowed an afternoon. The sole carpenter in the group was laughing the hardest. When the stories were done and the coffee was gone, they said farewell and walked to their cars.

Ryan climbed into the minivan, where his wife was waiting. Their infant son was already buckled in his car seat. Ryan was quiet. His wife looked at him.

"What is it?" she asked.

"Oh, the guys were talking about that story."

"The one from the sermon? About drywall?"

"Yeah." Ryan paused. "The story bothered me. I mean, the story was fine, and I guess it helped the sermon, but the truth is, I know more about Pastor Tim—his bad drywall skills, his two grandkids, his biking, his favorite hymns—than I do about most people. I'd love to hear a sermon where he doesn't talk about himself."

The Ease of Using Your Own Life

Early in the week, most of us know which passage we are preaching on Sunday. Maybe we've already met with the worship planning team and have a sense about where the service will go and how the sermon will fit. We've thought about songs or dramas or images that will be used in other parts of the service.

We then go through our week thinking about the passage. When we are at the gym. When we are getting groceries. When we are driving. Sitting at the dinner table. Leading a meeting. Watching a game. Because of this, the first filter the text goes through is our own lives: *What does this mean for me? Where do I see God work like this? What happened to me this week that illustrates this point?*

Preachers are sponges for anything that happens to us that could remotely connect with the sermon. While the benefit of this is that the ancient Word is linked to contemporary life, the danger is that the only contemporary life it's linked to is ours!

In a week packed with things to do, finding any illustration feels like a gift. The relief we feel at having the right story for the right text at the right time can lead us to use whatever we can find, even if the stories tend to be our own. But as Ryan showed in the opening story, this becomes wearying to a congregation. The sermon is no longer opening up a Scripture passage to apply it to the life of the congregation; instead it has become a testimony: this is what God did in my life this week.

The occasional testimony from a preacher is fine (and we'll talk about when later in this chapter). But using yourself and your life (or the lives of your spouse, children, nephews, nieces, etc.) as the main source of your illustrations may reveal a lack of creativity at best and laziness or self-centeredness at worst—or the belief that what happens in your family is more fascinating than the things that happen in the families of your parishioners.

> **People want to hear how the passage of Scripture applies to their lives, not ours. Our calling as preachers is to do that and to do it well.**

People want to hear how the passage of Scripture applies to their lives, not ours. Our calling as preachers is to do that and to do it well.

Work Your Way Up the Age Groups

All of us view life from our current vantage point. If we are forty-five years old, married, with two teenage children, we view life from that perspective. We know the challenges of resource management. We know the anxiety of having a child learn to drive. We have a list of questions for anyone who wants to date our kid.

But not everyone in our congregations is in that spot. Eight-year-olds have no idea about mortgages. Sixteen-year-olds don't understand the anxiety we have about their driving. Most grandparents have long accepted the spouses their children have married.

When we are working on a passage, we view it from our vantage point: what is this text like to a married forty-five-year-old with two kids? But if we only use examples from our vantage point, we miss large sections of our congregation.

A helpful practice can be to walk through the text from the perspective of the different age groups in your church. Imagine that you are preaching on "Do not steal" as part of a series on the Ten Commandments. Many, hopefully most, of the people in your church don't have a significant issue with stealing. The challenge with preaching this passage is to reveal that all of us fall short of obeying this command.

So think about this as if you were eight years old. What are the temptations for an eight-year-old? What things would an eight-year-old want to steal? Our first thought is of what we wanted to steal when we were eight: candy, someone else's bike, a dollar from Mom's purse. But eight-year-olds now may want someone else's video game, their scooter or $10 from Mom's purse. (Although I think they still want candy.)

- Teenagers may be tempted by the tablet in their neighbor's locker or the sweet headphones turned in to the school's lost and found: "Oh, yeah, those are mine."

- Twenty-somethings may want to swipe something as basic as mac and cheese from their roommate's cupboard, or something as significant as the expensive chemistry book from the campus bookstore.

- Thirty-year-olds may want to steal someone else's job. They may lack contentment in their work and finagle their way to get a promotion they know someone else deserves.

- Middle-age folks may be tempted to skimp on giving to church so they can save a little more in the college fund.

- Retired congregants may want to hoard their time and energy, stealing valuable wisdom and vision from the life of the church.

A walk through the age groups can also point to what stealing reveals: a lack of trust in God to provide what we need. That is a problem all ages face. By doing this exercise we find we have great examples of how we are all tempted to steal, and the preacher didn't have to use his own life at all.

What Is It Like to Be You?

Not all eight-year-olds are the same, of course, and not all teenagers are tempted by the latest technology. To have good illustrations that come from the lives of our congregants, we need to listen to their lives.

When we meet a parishioner for lunch or chat with them after a meeting, one of the questions we should have in the back of our minds is, *What is it like to be you?* It's tempting for us to *imagine* what it is like to be twenty-eight when we are fifty, black when we are white, single when we are married and female when we are male, but it's our calling to *learn* what that's like.

This is another place where the intersection of preaching and pastoral care is so valuable. If we know what is happening in the lives of our hearers, we can engage with the text on their behalf.

Most people arrive at church with their best faces forward. Maybe in your tradition it is customary for people to dress up for church. Maybe you have members who wash their cars on Saturday so their autos look good for church on Sunday. If people are putting on their best look for Sunday morning, they may also be tempted to hide the fact that their son recently was caught with pot, that they once again failed to conceive a child this month or that grief from a recent loss is spiraling into depression.

And maybe no one knows their pain.

Just as a walk through the different age groups can illuminate a passage, so can a walk through the different life situations of your people. You know your congregation. A great exercise is to flip through your church directory, and as you do, ask, *What is it like to be you?* This can give you prompts about the challenges church members are facing, the joys they are experiencing or the hopes they have for the future.

In your congregation you probably have people who are

- newly widowed
- un- or underemployed
- gay or lesbian, whether that's known publicly or not

- worried about money
- failing a class at school
- victims of domestic violence
- starting to date
- caring for elderly parents
- struggling with infertility

Reading this list can seem overwhelming, so we don't explicitly include examples from every group in every sermon. But it may be helpful to think about how a sermon about "being salt and light" may be heard by these different groups. Or a message on "Be doers of the word and not merely hearers," or "God is my rock." When we are in the thick of our research and writing, it is easy to use our own lives for material. But imagining the text through the experiences of our parishioners will lead to much richer preaching.

We do not need to know the intimate details of everyone's lives in order to preach to them, but naming common experiences of pain helps all of our members—and us—to see how God is meeting us in that pain. Because many of us hide our deepest pain, it can be profoundly comforting to have something we are struggling with named from the pulpit. This can remind our hearers that they are not alone, that others know what grief or addiction is like, and that God's presence and power apply to all.

Asking the question, *What is it like to be you?* not only helps us with individual sermons, it also helps us to plan sermon series. If your congregation is made up of many elderly widows, a series on marriage may not be the best choice. If your congregation has many young families, think about how the Beatitudes series would apply to them.

Knowing our listeners well allows us to view the text through their lives and show them that the God who acted in Scripture so long ago is the same God who is acting in their lives today. This is the heart of good preaching.

WHAT MEDIA ARE PEOPLE CONSUMING?

North American media can be a great target for many preachers. We can rail against the sex, violence and stupidity of television, movies and Internet channels till the sun goes down. Unfortunately, this often becomes another way we preach about ourselves and our tastes: "I know some of you watch [insert a TV show you don't like]. Is there any redeeming quality to this? I would never watch that show!"

Congregants get two takeaways from this: (1) Our preacher hates a show I watch, and (2) I need to hide the fact that I watch it.

> **Knowing our listeners well allows us to view the text through their lives and show them that the God who acted in Scripture so long ago is the same God who is acting in their lives today. This is the heart of good preaching.**

But here's the truth: our congregations watch *The Bachelorette*. They play video games. They surf the Internet. They watch cat videos. They know more about zombies than you do.

Our parishioners are consuming media all the time. While there is so much out there not to like, there are more important things to consider: Why do they watch it? What is the draw? What are our congregants finding in reality television, in their favorite crime drama or in that silly sitcom? What music do they like and why?

For our single members, for example, a regular TV program may feel more like community than church does—especially if they are active on social media while they watch. You may not be able to name the number-one pop song, but many of your members can sing all the words. And at the end of a long day, sometimes a silly comedy is just what the doctor ordered.

In my context I work with many students who love to play video games. We have actually had students who play so many hours of video games that it threatens their academic standing. For a long time this mystified me. I simply did not understand the appeal. But then I heard a lecture by someone who worked on video game design. He talked about how the best video games tell great stories, and players become characters in the story. "Many of us know what it's like to get lost in a good book. For gamers, it's the same. They can get lost in a great story."

Suddenly, I understood. My students loved to get lost in good stories. Add in the ability to control the outcome of a story, conquer enemies along the way and solve a complicated puzzle (all with amazing graphics that have come a long way since *Space Invaders*), and it made sense. I had been judging video games as giant time wasters because that was my perspective. Judging video games in my sermons was about me; it wasn't for my listeners. It didn't help them. However, it told them (1) Our pastor doesn't like video games, and (2) I will hide the fact that I play video games. This created a wedge in my ability to care well for my students.

Instead, I need to learn the best possible uses of video games, find the best possible examples, use the most relevant stories and work them into my sermons. My students are going to play video games. How do I help that part of their life connect with Scripture?

Most video games have an end in mind: win the game, solve the puzzle, conquer the enemy. It may take hours to do it, but there is a definite end in mind. There is a goal. And some players can become relentless about achieving that goal. If I talk about God's pursuit of them as relentless and compare it to their unyielding quest to get to the top level of a game they play, they will see the humor but also feel the connection—God is that focused on loving me.

Good and evil also play out in many games, and conquering evil involves finding the right weapons, developing more power and knowing the enemy's weaknesses. Any sermon about good and evil, the armor of God, the schemes of the enemy or how sin seeks to destroy us can use examples from these games. For those of us who don't play, a web search can give us enough information on the most popular games to make connections. (Under no circumstances should you present yourself as a gamer when you are not. Not only is this deceitful, but someone will invite you to play, and you will look silly.)

For those who love romantic comedies or romance novels (even the tame ones sold in Christian bookstores), the general appeal is that love wins in the end, that everything turns out okay or that everyone lives happily ever after. This is an old desire within us, which is why the genre has been around for so long. We can poke holes in the genre and remind our listeners that most people don't live happily ever after, but an alternative is that we use the genre and its emotional pull to connect to the gospel. God has promised that someday there will be no more mourning or crying or pain (Rev 21). The fairy-tale ending may not come true in this life, but it will come true. The desire we have for everyone to live happily ever after is actually God's desire too. Watching romantic comedies or enjoying fairy tales may set us up for disappointment in daily life if we place our hope there, but if we gently nudge people toward the truth of the gospel that underlies these stories, we turn their hopes not to finding the perfect person but to the kingdom life that will someday come to its fullness when Christ returns.

People often consume the media they do because it offers something they need: an escape, a laugh, a shared experience with people they like or the hope that good wins in the end. As preachers we can judge and condemn the media our members consume, or we can look for the redeeming qualities and seek to connect those to the gospel.

Our congregants are going to watch reality TV and surf the Internet and read grocery store novels. They know (most of them) the bad parts to some of these forms of media. How can we take the best possible parts of these things, put them in our sermons *and leave ourselves out*?

How Are You Stretching Your Own Imagination?

Of course, we consume media too. We are not immune to the pull to reality TV, suspenseful dramas or witty comedies. Often what we see gives us a great illustration for that week's sermon. The challenge is not to do that every week or your sermons become a review of everything you watched. Whenever we start a sermon with "I was watching ____ this week" we have placed ourselves in the sermon. People know what we watched and have learned something about us. Even the slight change in phrase helps: "[Name of show] is a television drama about detectives in New York City. In one episode . . ." The illustration then is about the show, not about your experience of watching the show.

As preachers we also want to keep stretching our imaginations. So much of we watch can do this. Many series are well-written, well-acted and make us think about the big questions of life: good versus evil, ethical choices, marital commitments, racial reconciliation, life and death. Great movies do the same.

We can also limit inserting our own stories into our sermons by knowing a lot of other stories. Television and films provide us with many stories. But so do great books. We preachers need to be reading deeply, widely and often.[1] When we read, we are forced to imagine what the author is describing: a hot courtroom in Georgia, the freshness of a mountain stream or the delighted squeal of child in a swing.

When we read we get different answers to the question, *What is it like to be you?* What was it like to be a female slave right before the Civil War? What is it like to lose someone to a terrorist attack? What is it like to give birth? What is it like to be you?

While we may mine the books and magazines we read for stories to place into our sermons, an additional benefit of reading is that it exposes us to stories not our own. We default to our own stories because we know them. But if we fill our minds with the stories of others, the temptation to use our own stories fades.

Another benefit of reading is that it stretches our vocabulary and animates our phrasing. Good writing shows us how language works, and we learn from a good novelist how to pair words, apply adjectives or devise similes that break open an idea. Just as we read the historic confessions of the church to shape our language for God, we read other voices to shape our language of human experience.

But we read for more than to know a good story and expand our rhetorical skills. We also read to know ourselves better. Eugene Peterson writes,

> I actively went looking for help to support me in maintaining and developing the integrity of my pastor/writer vocation. I was looking for a pastor, a priest, a guide—someone who could help me work out my calling in this uncongenial setting. . . . I made several attempts to find a vocational mentor from among the living, without success. Then I found Fyodor Dostoevsky.

I took my appointments calendar and wrote in two-hour meetings with "FD" three afternoons a week. Over the next seven months I read through the entire corpus, some of it twice.[2]

If you laugh at the idea of finding six hours each week to read, start with two. Write it in your appointments calendar and keep it. The goal is to keep your imagination fed and flourishing, and this rarely happens without intention. Joining a book club helps with this too, but even having a book buddy with whom you share your latest reads is a great way to keep reading.

Reading gives us a well of stories to draw from. Reading can help us think of people other than ourselves to put in our sermons; it helps us imagine how the text engages with the different people in our congregations; and it allows us to see God at work in all the varied settings of human life. The improvement of our vocabularies is a bonus.

Listening to well-told stories is also a way to hone our own skills. There are many podcasts available that tell good stories. Consider listening to stories during a run or while you drive as a way to improve your own storytelling ability and to give you more ideas for stories you can work into sermons.

When to Talk About You

There may be times when an illustration from our own lives seems perfect. How can we evaluate when to put ourselves in the sermon and when to leave ourselves out?

Here are some guidelines:

- *You are not the hero of the story.* You are not the one who gives $100 to the kid selling candy at the door. You do not save the puppy. You do not reference your daily practice of rising at 4 a.m., praying for two hours and then going for a five-mile run. If the experience makes you look better than you are and is not something that could happen to almost anyone, do not use it. The sermon is not about you.

- *The story points to God.* If you tell a story about your life, the goal of the story is to reveal something about God. What is God up to in your life and how can knowing that benefit your congregation? This is the sole reason to use a story about yourself.

- *You maintain the pastoral role that your context needs.* Some of us are known as "Reverend" whether we are at the council meeting or the car dealership. Telling a story that makes you look particularly foolish could be as dangerous as telling one that makes you the hero, because your congregants need you to be "Reverend." Psychologists tell us that some healthy transference is needed in certain roles within a community, and in many of our communities our people need us to be the pastor—someone who appears to love God and follow him well, not someone who is inclined to anger or foolish acts. Don't tell a story on yourself that could damage this. If the story is gently self-deprecating, humble and allows you to give testimony to God's work in your life, you're probably fine.

- *You do not overshare.* I was present when a young preacher told a long story in his sermon about his struggles with sex when he was in college. The discomfort in the sanctuary was palpable. That same discomfort arises when we tell a story that makes someone in our family (parents, spouse, child) look bad. The power of the story is lost in the anxiety people have about your embarrassment (or lack of it) or the troubles you have in your family. If you were to share such a story in a small group, people could speak back to you about the way the story affected them. But in a worship setting this is almost impossible. You give them a hard thing to hold when you overshare, and they have nowhere to go with it.

A FINAL CHALLENGE

A good corrective to the problem of putting yourself in the sermon is to see how many sermons you can preach without mentioning yourself at all. If you write a manuscript, use the search tool and look for the word *I*. If you have an extensive outline, comb through your illustrations and delete any that are self-referential.

One of my seminary professors once said, "Preaching is a narcissistic activity. We have a few hundred people in a room and we expect them to listen to us talk and to do what we say." Our challenge—our calling—is to make preaching less about us and more about God. As John the Baptist said, "He must increase, but I must decrease" (Jn 3:30).

> **Our challenge—our calling—is to make preaching less about us and more about God.**

We don't want our sermons to teach people about us. We want our sermons to point to God and his grace. We want our parishioners to walk away knowing God better and loving him more. When we let ourselves and our stories fade, the brightness of the gospel story shines through.

ten

Getting Feedback About Your Preaching

You know how it goes. You've just spent yourself preaching a sermon. Your brow is sweaty. Your body is jazzed by adrenaline and completely exhausted. The service is over. You make your way to the back of the church to shake hands as people leave, or you stand in the lobby nursing a cup of coffee. And now, after you have worked hard for a week and crossed the finish line, this is what you hear: "Good morning." "Good morning." "Nice service today." "Nice to see you." "Good morning."

I had one parishioner who broke the mold. A preacher himself who was serving as a chaplain in a local hospital, he would come to me each week, shake my hand and offer a very specific compliment about the sermon: "I really loved that insight about Thomas being a twin and how that impacted his understanding of identity." "Your structure was so clear today: God did this for them and this is how he does that for us." "That story about swimming with your nephew was perfect!"

You know whom I was most eager to see after every sermon? Him. Here was someone who was listening well, and who saw it as his call to affirm me week in and week out. But he was also trained in the art of preaching. He knew what to listen for, and he knew what to tell me.

When most laypeople are asked what makes for a good sermon, the answers run along these lines: a good sermon is funny, short, interesting, teaches me something, isn't boring, doesn't use long words, applies to my life.

However, the standards for how preachers evaluate sermons are shaped by what we may have been taught in seminary. When preachers speak about sermons, we talk about exegesis, hermeneutics, theology, sermon structure and use of Scripture. "Funny" or "interesting" are good qualities to have, but most preachers don't hold those out as goals of the sermon, because we have been taught to think and speak very differently about the work of preaching.

Think of it this way: a sermon is like an iceberg—most of the work is below the surface. What congregants see on Sunday morning is a small part of the whole. In the days leading up to Sunday, we have read the passage several times, studied it in its original language, read commentaries, listed ideas, prayed, drafted outlines, started writing, written some more, prayed some more, edited what was written, read the written work out loud, honed the words, read it out loud again, maybe memorized much of the message, practiced movements and gestures, prayed again and practiced some more so that when Sunday morning comes what is visible has a strong foundation.

And this is where the mismatch begins. We've been thinking about the message for hours. The person in the pew listens for twenty-two minutes.

Form? Structure? Good exegesis? Most parishioners enter into the worship space glad to have found a parking spot. The children fought in the minivan the whole way there. She noticed another gray hair this morning. He's wondering what lunch will be at the retirement home. Is that ache in my midsection a problem? Did I remember the peanut-free cookies for Sunday school? What's that guy's name again? Darrell? Dylan? Who has the offering?

Between shepherding children into a seat, getting a bulletin, seeing who's there, feeling their age as they lower themselves into a pew, reading the announcements (Katie, you have nursery duty today!) and simply shifting gears from the rest of life to the life of corporate worship, few parishioners have the mental energy needed to listen well. So what do they hear? They hear the funny, the interesting, the new, the story or the application.

When a listener doesn't know the difference between *homiletic* and *hermeneutic*, and we preachers aren't necessarily focused on being funny or interesting, we need some help in talking with each other about preaching.

The truth is, preachers and parishioners have the same goal: that the Word of God will come alive in the hearts and minds of all who hear it by the power of the Holy Spirit, who uses preaching to animate all of us for grateful service in the kingdom of God.

The truth is, preachers and parishioners have the same goal: that the Word of God will come alive in the hearts and minds of all who hear it by the power of the Holy Spirit, who uses preaching to animate all of us for grateful service in the kingdom of God.

So how do we get there?

By talking about preaching. By talking *well* about preaching. By laying down our egos and our arrogance, our laziness and our fear of conflict, and actually engaging the topic.

The Vulnerability of the Preacher

"I could not believe how exhausted I was!" The first-time preacher was standing in my office doorway, talking about her Sunday. "I went out to my car and had to summon the energy to drive home. It was as if I had run ten miles!"

Another new preacher, an older student who enjoyed a long career as a beloved teacher, slumped in my office after his first classroom sermon had not been what he wanted. "I've taught for years, I am used to being up in front of people . . ." He fell silent for several seconds. "This was unlike anything I've ever done."

After twenty years of preaching, I am still amazed at what preaching demands. Thoughtful engagement of Scripture. A prayerful life. A deep love of the people you are preaching to. Engaging, relevant illustrations. Life-changing application. And all of this done with a delivery that keeps people not only awake but interested.

Add to this the spiritual dimension that those who preach are at the same time the mouthpiece of God and the object of the enemy's attacks, and a mere mortal can quickly become overwhelmed.

In the winter of 1982, author and pastor Frederick Buechner accepted an invitation to teach preaching for a term in Harvard Divinity School. He writes,

> I had never understood so clearly before what preaching is to me. Basically, it is to proclaim a Mystery before which, before whom, even our most exalted ideas turn to straw. It is also to proclaim this Mystery with a passion that ideas alone have little to do with. It is to try to put the Gospel into words not the way you would compose an essay but the way you would write a poem or a love letter—putting your heart into it, your own excitement, most of all your own life.[1]

This is why it can be so hard to talk about our preaching—our very identities and callings can seem to be wrapped up in how we preach.

We love good sermons. We believe they matter. Many of us can name sermons that corrected us, comforted us or stretched our imaginations in ways they needed to be stretched. We can read a passage of Scripture and recall an illustration from a sermon preached on that same passage years before that still rings within us. Most of us go into worship expecting that the sermon will do something—teach, encourage, challenge, convict.

But we preachers are humans. Trained, often; experienced, sometimes. But each preacher is still a human whose child may have been sick in the middle of the night, or who had a funeral and four nights away from his family this week, or who herself is struggling with God right now and finds it very hard to stand up and preach.

The high demands on the preaching event are a perfect storm: God can do amazing things or it can be twenty-two minutes of pain for preacher and parishioner alike. (These things are not mutually exclusive—God, thankfully, is not limited by the skills of the preacher.) But preaching is a unique practice, wholly demanding and yet routine. Holy and human. Exhausting and exhilarating. It will take everything you have. Knowing this, how do we help preachers and parishioners talk about preaching?

My colleague sighed at me across the table. She picked up a chip, dipped it in the salsa and said, "I spend hours poring over the text, coming up with illustrations, trying to make it clear as well as interesting, and what I hear most as the people are walking out is 'Have a good morning.'" She took a bite, chewed for a moment, swallowed and then said, "Is it too much to ask for someone to say something helpful?"

Like my colleague, most of us welcome thoughtful engagement with our sermons—it is how we improve! And most of us really do want to improve. We have no interest in boring our congregations or teaching them things that aren't helpful or using illustrations that don't connect. We really do want to know how our preaching is being received.

But here's another admission: we preachers are like peaches; we bruise easily. As Frederick Buechner said, we put our hearts, our excitement and most of all our own lives into our preaching. It can be hard to receive critique on something that feels as if it is a very part of our beings.

Prepare Yourself

So before you read any further, ask yourself, *Am I ready for this? Am I ready to hear what people want to tell me about my preaching? Am I secure in my calling to preach? Do I have a healthy relationship with this church? Do we like each other?*

And then there is this question: *Am I willing to change?* You're reading this book, so that's one sign that you are. But reading a book and tweaking some things on our own is more fun: we get to choose what we want to work on, and we get to say whether we're getting better.

Once you move into intentional conversations with your congregation about your preaching, they are actually going to start looking for things to change! Suddenly you'll have 12 or 50 or 150 or 500 people listening for any improvement. Preaching then feels like taking a fashion-conscious sixteen-year-old to the mall as a shopping consultant: no, not that, try this, are you sure about that color, that is the wrong cut for your hips. Yikes!

Remember Where They're Coming From

Your parishioners watch you stand up front, week after week, and do something that most of them would never want to do. They also know you have been trained, have been taught, have been at this craft for a while—so what can they offer? What can they say? Even if they know that something is off, they may not know how to say it.

In many communities the preacher is seen as "other." You are viewed as holier, wiser, more pious and closer to God. It can feel very intimidating for a parishioner to speak with you about the need for new carpet in the nursery, let alone come up with something helpful to say about preaching. The pressure on a parishioner to speak into this very tender area of your life can be too much to bear. Add to this any cultural context that puts the preacher on an additional pedestal (an Asian student of mine reported her shock at seeing her pastor enter the restroom!), and talking about preaching may never happen.

This may be a challenge for whichever group has official oversight of the preaching ministry of your church (in most churches this is the responsibility of the elders or board). The members of this group may be accountants, architects, teachers, business leaders, work-at-home parents—each one skilled at what they do, but they aren't sure how to talk with the preacher about preaching.

The members of the group may also have different opinions and different priorities. They listen differently to the same sermons. They may want different texts or topics addressed. So the group entrusted with the responsibility to speak to the pastor about preaching may be unsure about how to proceed or whose opinions matter most.

Imagine this scene:

Setting: Executive committee meeting of the elders; First Community Church. Basement room, smell of coffee in the air, children's art on the walls.

Chair   We need to do the annual evaluation of Pastor's preaching.

(mild groaning)

Elder 1   I don't know what to say.

Elder 2   It's fine. It's not great, but it's fine.

Elder 3   I can't hear another illustration about _____ [golf, Pinterest, bicycling, *Lord of the Rings*, baking].

(heads nodding; chuckling)

Elder 1   I don't think it's "fine." My kids never listen.

Elder 2   We aren't going to fire our pastor for it. It's not _____ [Tim Keller, Marva Dawn, Will Willimon, Barbara Brown Taylor, Chuck Swindoll, Andy Stanley, popular local preacher], but it's okay.

Elder 1   It's not okay.

Chair   What's not okay about it? What would you like to tell the pastor?

(silence)

Elder 1   *(sigh)* I would like to say: preach to my kids. If my kids listen, I'll listen.

Elder 3   That's true. And maybe ask for more Old Testament. Fewer topical sermons.

Elder 2   Well, now that I'm thinking about it, I'd love to hear something on _____ [Revelation, money management, life after death, parenting].

Chair   Good ideas here. Who wants to join me at breakfast with Pastor in a week to discuss these things?

(silence)

Elder 1   I'll go.

Chair   Good, that's settled then. Moving on to other business . . .

The elders are fulfilling the letter of the law. They will have breakfast with their pastor and list these ideas and concerns. Their pastor will listen. And on the drive back to the office after the oatmeal, toast and coffee, the pastor will be thinking, *What does it mean to preach to the kids? Do they want a children's sermon every week? A few weeks ago I mentioned Nintendo. Thought that would connect with the kids. What about lectionary preaching? Do they notice? Do they know what it is? I should have taken that Old Testament preaching elective in seminary. Did they say anything about the gospel? Are they hearing the gospel in my preaching? Maybe I should ask that question. Maybe I should have asked more questions. I really don't know what they want.*

And then, over two suppers that evening:

Elder 1's spouse   How was breakfast with the pastor?

Elder 1   Fine. I asked for sermons that the kids would listen to.

Elder 1's spouse   Great. Hope that was heard.

. . . . .

Pastor's spouse   How was breakfast with the elders?

Pastor   Fine. I'm thinking about a series on Exodus.

Pastor's spouse   Huh. That'd be good.

As we can see, what was said and what was heard were very different things. The result is that neither party will be satisfied with where they go from here.

Create a Feedback Loop

The long-term goal is to create a better feedback loop from the congregation to you about your preaching, and from you back to them.

An initial exercise. The first thing may be to talk about what preaching is. You also want to start slowly and in the safest possible way for all involved. (You don't want to be skewered, and they don't want to hurt you.) Talking about preaching in general is a good on-ramp to a more personal conversation.

Because you and your hearers may have different ideas about the goals of preaching and what makes for a good sermon, you may want to start with a simple exercise. This is something that the elders, the worship committee or the youth group could each do in a short amount of time. The goal is to get people thinking about preaching in general, not for them at this point to talk about your preaching specifically. You may get the best results if the chair of the group leads them through this exercise in your absence and then collects the responses to give to you. The respondents may also be helped if they know that the worship committee or the elders are asking, and not you.

You may want to complete the exercise yourself before handing it out to anyone else. Asking ourselves what the goal of preaching is leads to clarity about what we are trying to do!

Here's the exercise:

Finish these sentences:

1. What God does through preaching is . . .

2. One of the best sermons I ever heard was . . .

3. I don't listen as well during a sermon when . . .

4. What I listen for most in a sermon is . . .

5. One thing God taught me through preaching is . . .

Each group could be encouraged to discuss their results with each other after completing the sentences, and one person could take notes of the conversation and pass them on to you.

While the exercise is intentionally not about your preaching, it should give you insight into how your people are listening to your sermons.

Widen the conversation. After you've gathered this data, review it and look for themes. Does anything come up repeatedly? Does anything excite you? Does anything trouble you?

You could stop right here. Maybe you have enough general information that can inform a few changes you may want to make. Maybe you want to talk more about preaching in general with your worship committee or elders.

If you're ready to make it less general (about preaching) and more specific (about *your* preaching), think about how the information gained from the previous questions can inform what you need to focus on next. While the process laid out here may seem overwhelming, you are free to adapt it to your context and your needs. The goal is to keep improving and to get some help with that from the people who listen to your sermons. You can use what follows to serve your own congregation well.

Confidential small group. For this next step, you may be served by bringing the conversation to a different group.

Many congregations have a small group of people who serve as the pastor-church relations team or the pastor's support group. These are people specifically chosen because of their spiritual maturity, spiritual gifts of encouragement and wisdom, and their ability to keep matters in confidence—even from their spouses.

If you don't have such a group, think about starting one. You only need two to four people, and you can choose people you like and trust. Invite them by saying something like "I have learned I can trust you with some really hard things, and you give great advice. I'm thinking about trying something related to my preaching ministry, and I'd love to have your counsel." Most people will be honored that you have asked and eager to help. (You can even start by meeting with one person and asking that person about your preaching. One trusted adviser who has your best interests at heart can really help.)

If you already have such a group, they would be perfect to ask about how your preaching is being received. Share with them what you learned from the short exercise and ask them where they think you need to grow as a preacher. Where would the congregation be best served? What things am I overlooking? If there is one thing I could do better, what is it?

This may be enough for now. Keeping the conversation in this group may give you the prompts you need to work toward steady improvement.

Preparing a feedback form. The confidential small group could assist you in developing a feedback form. (A web search for "sermon feedback form" will provide you with several models.) As you do so, ponder what would be most helpful to you as the preacher. What questions would you most like to ask? Questions about delivery, illustrations or grace? Look back over the chapters of this book. Do any chapters name something you hope to improve?

As you prepare the form, avoid calling it an "evaluation" form. This isn't a way for listeners to grade the sermon. This is a way to foster conversations about your preaching in a way that is most healthy for the church. Have the members of your confidential small group try out the feedback form and see how it aids them in listening to the sermon, and how it aids you in preparing for and delivering your message. (The form should have easily understood questions and should be easy to complete during the time it takes to receive the offering.)

Once you've developed a draft feedback form and the small group is using it, you may want to keep the conversation within this group for a while. It's a risk to ask people—even people we love and trust—to assess something as intimate to us as our preaching. If you are getting good feedback and this group is very helpful, give time to the project. Let your emotional resilience around this topic strengthen before you move on to the elders, council, board or congregation. You may (and should!) let the group that oversees you know that you are doing this work with your small team of advisers. But allow yourself the time you need to prepare before making the conversation more public.

Again, if this is as far as you want to go right now, that's fine.

Official body. When you're ready to take the next step, invite someone from your small group to join the next meeting of the group of people who are entrusted with supervision of the preaching ministry of the church (board, elders, etc.). The member of the small group can describe the conversations the group has been having and the work they've been doing.

The small-group representative can distribute the most recent draft of the feedback form to the elders. (Put the word *Draft* on the top of the form, which will remind readers that their input is welcome.) That person can teach the elders about the different questions on the form, why they were chosen and how they have been helpful to you as their preacher.

Suggest to the elders that the next step is for them (all of them if your elder group is small, or a handful of them if you have many elders) to use the form during a worship service. They will be using the form to give you feedback, but they will also be evaluating the form itself on its ease of use.

For four weeks the first group of elders will use the form. At the next meeting they will give feedback on the form to the small group. The small group can edit the form as suggested, and then the next group of elders can try the beta version.

Congregation. Along with your elders, think about how to involve the congregation. Just about everyone in the congregation will want to be involved because everyone has an opinion about preaching. Think about how to do this strategically: who should be asked, how, and what will be done with the forms when they are collected?

You can start small by asking the seventh and eighth grade students to be the first from the congregation to use the form for one Sunday, for example. Visit their Sunday school class or youth group (perhaps with someone from your small group) and ask them to help you out. Give them the form and see if they have any questions. After the sermon meet with them again and see what it was like for them. If the model works, try it again with the senior citizen's group, men's Bible study, mothers of preschoolers or high school youth group.

When you are ready to invite everyone, you could place an announcement in the bulletin (or in the church's email or on the screen during announcement time) that reads something like this:

Sermon Feedback: The elders and Pastor Donnelly have developed a feedback form to foster good conversations about preaching. A group of people [or households, elder districts, etc.] will be selected for Advent and again in Lent [or November and March] to use the form for that season. We hope to hear from a variety of the members over the next year. The elders will notify you when you've been selected [or sign up in the back of church or online]. All contributions will be confidential. [Name of elder] is coordinating the process, and you can contact her with any questions. Thank you for serving the church in this way!

Once you have the completed forms, you need to read them. This sounds obvious, but how many of us would love to leave it right here? This is where your small group can help. Have them gather the forms and collate the answers into one document. This way they can also maintain the confidentiality of the process. They can meet with you and go over the results together. They can also help you think about where to go from here. A colleague who is an experienced college professor and undergoes twice-a-year evaluations of his teaching suggests throwing out the top 10 percent and the bottom 10 percent, and paying attention to common themes in the rest. That keeps us from being overly critical or narcissistic about evaluations—that is, it keeps us from giving undue attention to the outliers.

SUGGESTED TIMELINE FOR CONGREGATIONAL INVOLVEMENT

What follows is one possible way to move through this process. Feel free to amend any of this to suit your context.

Outline for Creating a Feedback Loop (with Suggested Timeline)

1. Have a conversation with supervising body about the process (month 1)

2. Gather general data from a few groups using exercise above (months 2-4)

3. Gather confidential small group (months 5-7, or as long as needed)

   a. Review data from exercise

   b. Consider areas for growth (in what the congregation can learn about preaching and what you can learn about how they listen)

   c. Develop draft of feedback form

4. Meet with supervising body (give monthly updates prior to this; set intentional meeting after month 6 or when ready)

   a. Review data from exercise

   b. Review work of small group

   c. Review draft of feedback form

5. Develop plan (months 8-9)

   a. Elders (either all of them or a small group of them)

      1. Use feedback form for four weeks

      2. Review usefulness of form as well as sermons at next meeting

   b. Different group of elders or worship committee

      1. Use feedback form for four weeks

      2. Review usefulness of form as well as sermons at next meeting

   c. Develop final version of feedback form

   d. Invite different groups to review sermons for each liturgical season or sermon series using final draft of feedback form; as you invite people, think about diversity in age, background, education, interest, culture, etc.

OTHER WAYS TO GET PEOPLE INVOLVED

Because preaching is a shared activity (one person preaches, but we all listen), you may also want to think of ways to get people involved in preparing the sermon. This can be done even if you don't do any of the previous steps! There are ways to get people interested in preaching without the additional work and stress of developing a feedback system, and involving others in sermon preparation will generate natural opportunities for feedback.

I have a colleague who enjoys "Brown Bag and Bible" every week. He intentionally chooses a handful of people to eat lunch with him and talk about the preaching text for that week. They offer suggestions, stories and questions, and he weaves those contributions into the sermon. Then when they come on Sunday they are invested in the sermon and eager to hear it. This pastor rotates the members of the group every few months to be sure all voices of the church are represented. The practice has led to a much greater interest in the sermon-writing process and in the preaching event.

One church does something similar, but hosts a meal on a weekday evening and invites anyone to come—members, neighbors, skeptics. The group reads the week's text and anyone can say or ask anything they wish. The sermon responds to what is raised at the meal, including the skeptical comments.

Using adult education classes that follow the worship service to discuss the sermon is another way of teaching the details that couldn't be included in the sermon, and indirectly receiving sermon feedback.

One of the best experiences I had occurred when I was teaching eleventh and twelfth grade church school. I was starting a new sermon series on the book of Ruth and asked my students if they'd like to have copies of the sermons after I preached them, and we could go over them together. They were very interested, so each

Sunday I would preach and then we would gather and go over the Scripture passage and the sermon. I was able to teach them about the rest of the "iceberg"—the things I couldn't include in the sermon. I gave them copies of the Hebrew-English interlinear Bible, and we learned about the text's words and grammar. We learned how the story of Ruth fits into the larger narrative of Scripture. They asked me great questions about the decisions I had to make as a preacher concerning what to include and what to leave out. Then we would look ahead to the next passage and brainstorm ideas. As a result, they listened more intently to my sermons, and I was always thinking of them while I wrote.

Another preacher has the "Idea Hopper," which is simply a shoebox with a slit through the lid. If someone has an idea for a sermon, a passage they'd like to hear preached, an article they found interesting or even a comic strip about church, they put it in the hopper. They can also email ideas and put "Idea Hopper" in the subject line.

Your parishioners are genuinely interested in your preaching. They want the best for you and for the church. Creating a feedback loop that gives everyone ways to have good conversations about preaching helps your church move toward health.

If your church has implemented a feedback loop, if you are starting to hear specific, positive comments about your sermon or even if you simply started a "Brown Bag and Bible" group, say thank you. Put an announcement in the bulletin thanking each group that has helped you.

IF YOU'RE MARRIED: HOW TO TALK ABOUT SERMONS WITH YOUR SPOUSE

Right after a sermon is done (and up to two days after) I'm not ready to hear from my beloved about what he thought. The experience is too fresh, and honestly I'm still thinking of all the things I wish could have been different. I probably know it wasn't my best sermon (how many of those are there?), and I'm tired from preaching and not in great space to hear a critique.

My spouse, however, needed to be told this. I couldn't assume that he would figure it out. I actually had to say words. Out loud. To him. I think I said something like, "Hey, there's no way you would know this without me telling you, but after I'm done preaching I really need you to simply say I did well. In a day or two you can say, 'I'm still thinking about your sermon and have a question,' but I can't respond to that right after preaching. I'm too tender and too tired."

People who are newly married or new to preaching may want to be clear with their spouse about what they need and when they need it. Preachers who have been married for several years, who have been preaching for several years or who have served multiple congregations may learn to lean on their spouse for preaching responses as she or he is the person who has listened to them for the longest time and can often provide helpful feedback.

But it's also perfectly fine to not speak about your sermons with your spouse at all. Marriages are complicated enough without giving your spouse the role of sermon evaluator every week. If you're honest, what you really want your spouse to say is, "That was the most moving sermon I've ever heard. It was smart and funny and insightful and brought me into the presence of God. It made me so honored—humbled, really—to be married to you."

That's not going to happen.

It is perfectly fine to let your elders do the evaluating and let your spouse simply be your spouse. You may need to wean both of you off of this if you've done it for years, but I think you'll both find Sundays to be much more enjoyable.

The key is first to discover what works for your marriage and second to see if it improves your preaching.

Receive It Well

When feedback comes our way—whether from a spouse, a small group or the church's leadership—it is so tempting to write it off: most of your members didn't go to Bible college or seminary, so what do they know about preaching? The truth is, they know enough to help us get better!

We need to be active listeners. If your group comes back with something you don't understand, ask for clarification. "Help me understand this comment" is a great way to invite your small group to aid you in receiving the feedback well.

Let's be honest: there is a lot of ego in our preaching. If we want to get better, we have to admit that we aren't perfect.

As my friend Ryan said, "If a sermon falls in a forest and no one can understand it, does it make a sermon? No." If the feedback consistently says that people are confused, bored or uninspired by our preaching, we can't argue that our preaching is clear, exciting or inspiring. We need to listen.

Humble yourself before the feedback you get, and you'll find that the benefits come not only in the preaching but also in your relationship to the church. They will know that you listen to them and take them seriously. That will help them listen to you and to take you seriously. Good things will come as a result.

Conclusion

We have covered a lot of ground together! Here's a good checklist to review as we consider whether our preaching is indeed getting better by Sunday.

- *Biblical preaching.* Was the text used to point people to God or to prove something you wanted to say?

- *God-centered preaching.* What has today's sermon taught your listeners about the triune God?

- *Grace-full preaching.* Did you tell them what to do or tell them what God has done and how we get to live differently because of it?

- *Compelling preaching.* If your listeners had to put your sermon in one sentence, could they do it?

- *Imaginative preaching.* If you used an image or prop to pull the sermon together, could a seventh-grade student remember the image *and* link it back to the text that was preached?

- *Contextual preaching.* What deep needs of *these* people on *this* day did the sermon address?

- *Relevant preaching.* Did the sermon answer this question: What does God do in our lives if this story is true?

- *Embodied preaching.* If you courageously were to watch this sermon via video, what do you guess you would want to change about your delivery? After you've watched the video: did you guess right?

- *Self-less preaching.* Did you avoid any self-promotion in this sermon?

- *Getting feedback about your preaching.* If you were to take one step toward getting helpful feedback about this sermon, what would it be?

None of us will hit each of these perfectly every Sunday. Thankfully, God extends his grace to preachers too! There are few tasks in ministry more demanding or rewarding than preaching. But as I said in the introduction, there is nothing we would rather spend our lives getting right because we believe that God uses preaching to change lives!

So in the moments when you wonder if your work makes a difference, remember this: God is always up to something. Your faithful labor, week in and week out, to bring the good news to hurting people is not in vain. Whenever you dwell in the Word, focus on God and preach grace, God is drawing people into the core of the gospel. When you preach compelling and relevant messages in a warm and engaging style, God is glorified. When you humble yourself to receive feedback from those who listen, you are imitating the humility of Jesus. When you preach well, we see Christ because of you!

I tell my students that if they see me in a pew some Sunday when they step up to preach, they need to imagine me wearing face paint and holding a cowbell—I am the biggest fan in the room! I am not evaluating their sermon in that moment. I am cheering them on.

I hope this book cheers you on in the beautiful, hard work of writing and delivering sermons. Preaching is a great privilege, holy work, and I believe that God uses it to change people, change the church and change the world. Keep it up. Do not grow weary. God is doing amazing things in you and in your church. Preach the Word, preach it with grace, and keep your eyes open. You'll get better and better at spotting what God is up to. I'm praying that we all do.

So even if I'm not in your pew this Sunday, imagine me in the front row, cheering you on to do this holy work in the best way you can. May God bless all of us who preach, using us to shape his church and build his kingdom. To God alone be the glory!

Acknowledgments

Every book is the product of a group of people. That has become abundantly clear to me as I have worked on this one.

The good people at InterVarsity Press took a risk on me, and I am so grateful for their willingness to do so! It is a joy to be associated with a publishing house that seeks to love the church by equipping its pastors.

God has placed me smack dab in the middle of an amazing group of people who are not only my friends but also intelligent, funny, great writers and incredibly kind. Each of these people read the manuscript and offered feedback that was both keen and generous. To a person they wrote witty comments in the margins, providing me with good laughter as I worked. I wish for you a group of friends like these: David Beelen, Joy Bonnema, Andrea Bult, Randy Buursma, Laura De Jong, Scott Hoezee, Meg Jenista, Neal Plantinga, Matt Postma, Robert Nordling, Kurt Schaefer and Ryan Struyck. Thank you all.

Mark Labberton generously agreed to write the foreword, and I'm so honored that he did. Thank you, Mark.

My discernment group prayed me through: David Beelen, Joy Bonnema, Cherith Fee Nordling, Robert Nordling and Shirley Hoogstra. Thank you for cheering me on and sending me notes that said things like, "Woo hoo! DUDE! This chapter is awesome!" Stars in your crowns, people.

The five amazing people who make up the Dershem family—Aric, Marie, Hannah, Anton and Christian—have provided me with more joy (and food!) over the years than any one person deserves. I love you, guys!

As proof of God's creative genius, redemptive power and sustaining grace, God brought Andrew Kromminga into my life. Drew is a true partner in life, a champion of my gifts and a lover of the work I am called to do. Many Saturday mornings he made me a good breakfast so I could go up to my office and write. Many weekday evenings he listened as I worked through a knot I was untangling with the book. He read the manuscript—twice! When I find his face in the congregation as I am preaching, he is beaming. Even when I am preaching about sin. That's love.

Appendix

Resources for Inspiration and Education

There are so many resources that could be listed here. I've selected ones that I've found particularly helpful and given some reasons why.

Books About Preaching and Public Speaking

Carrell, Lori. *The Great American Sermon Survey*. Wheaton, IL: Mainstay Church Resources, 2000.

Fascinating data on how people listen to sermons and why sermons are unique public speaking events.

———. *Preaching That Matters: Reflective Practices for Transforming Sermons*. Herndon, VA: Alban Institute, 2013.

In her research Dr. Carrell learned that the preacher's spiritual life has the biggest impact on transformational preaching. Because of that, she designed retreats to help preachers revive their spiritual lives, and this is the workbook derived from those retreats. An excellent book to use with a small group or a mentor.

Chappell, Bryan. *Christ-Centered Preaching*. Grand Rapids: Baker, 1994.

How can we preach God's grace *and* inspire human action? Chappell tackles this good question.

Greidanus, Sidney. *The Modern Preacher and the Ancient Text*. Grand Rapids: Eerdmans, 1988.

A resource that can help you engage more deeply with the biblical text, bridging the gap from then to now.

Heath, Chip, and Dan Heath. *Made to Stick: Why Some Ideas Survive and Others Die*. New York: Random House, 2007.

A very practical guide for anyone who wants to create memorable presentations: simple, unexpected, concrete, credible, emotional stories. Easy to read, entertaining and easily applicable to preaching.

Hoezee, Scott. *Actuality: Real Life Stories for Sermons That Matter*. Artistry of Preaching Series. Nashville: Abingdon, 2014.

A great antidote to canned illustrations. Rev. Hoezee helps preachers find and tell great stories.

Jacks, Robert. *Getting the Word Across: Speech Communication for Pastors and Lay Leaders*. Grand Rapids: Eerdmans, 1995.

A handbook with vocal exercises specifically designed for preachers. A great tool for keeping your voice in shape. This can also help lay readers or drama leaders in your church.

———. *Just Say the Word*: *Writing for the Ear*. Grand Rapids: Eerdmans, 1981.

If you write out your sermons so you can preach from a manuscript, Jacks offers very helpful ways to write for the ear rather than the eye. His advice also makes it easier to deliver a written manuscript.

Jonker, Peter. *Preaching in Pictures: Using Images for Sermons That Connect*. Artistry of Preaching Series. Nashville: Abingdon, 2015.

If you want memorable sermons, use strong images. Rev. Jonker walks preachers through the process of finding strong images and weaving them into sermons.

Piper, John. *The Supremacy of God in Preaching*. Grand Rapids: Baker, 2004.

An inspiring reminder that every sermon is about God—not the preacher, not the method, not the latest news. Piper also teaches readers about great preachers of the past.

Plantinga, Cornelius, Jr. *Reading for Preaching: The Preacher in Con-*

versation with Storytellers, Biographers, Poets, and Journalists. Grand Rapids: Eerdmans, 2013.

What should we be reading, and how can what we read inform our preaching? A wonderful writer himself, Plantinga steers us toward other authors who can help us think about grace and truth.

Robinson, Haddon. *Biblical Preaching.* Grand Rapids: Baker, 2001.

A classic. If you need help whittling a sermon down to one big idea, Robinson is your guide.

Taylor, Barbara Brown. *The Preaching Life.* Lanham, MD: Rowman & Littlefield, 1993.

A memoir about preaching that is beautifully written and will have you thinking that she knows your life from the inside out.

Wilson, Paul Scott. *The Four Pages of a Sermon.* Nashville: Abingdon, 1999.

Wilson helps us cull a strong outline from messy Scripture passages and develop sermons that move our listeners from trouble to grace. If you're not sure how to preach grace, read Wilson.

———. *The Practice of Preaching.* Rev. ed. Nashville: Abingdon, 2007.

A more developed application of *The Four Pages*, with a step-by-step guide to writing a sermon.

BOOKS ABOUT PASTORING

Braestrup, Kate. *Here If You Need Me: A True Story.* New York: Little, Brown, 2007.

Braestrup tells the story of her later-in-life call to seminary and then of her work as a chaplain with the Maine Warden Service, serving game wardens and the people in crisis they are called to help.

Dawn, Marva. *The Sense of the Call: A Sabbath Way of Life for Those Who Serve God, the Church, and the Word.* Grand Rapids: Eerdmans, 2006.

We all need help discerning the important from the urgent. Practicing sabbath is a way to learn this, and Dr. Dawn winsomely invites us to rest, cease, feast and embrace.

Lischer, Richard. *Open Secrets: A Spiritual Journey Through a Country Church.* New York: Doubleday, 2001.

A memoir of his early years pastoring a rural church. Every rookie pastor will relate to these stories.

Peterson, Eugene. *The Contemplative Pastor: Returning to the Art of Spiritual Direction*. Grand Rapids: Eerdmans, 1980.

———. *Five Smooth Stones for Pastoral Work*. Grand Rapids: Eerdmans, 1990.

———. *The Pastor: A Memoir*. New York: HarperOne, 2011.

———. *Under the Unpredictable Plant: An Exploration in Vocational Holiness*. Grand Rapids: Eerdmans, 1980.

———. *Working the Angles: The Shape of Pastoral Integrity*. Grand Rapids: Eerdmans, 1987.

I try to read one of these books every year. Four of these books are short and engaging. They would be great to read with another pastor or mentor, or in a clergy small group. Peterson's memoir is thick with wisdom.

Books About Dwelling in the Word

Olesburg, Lindsey. *The Bible Study Handbook: A Comprehensive Guide to an Essential Practice*. Downers Grove, IL: InterVarsity Press, 2012.

A practical and inviting resource for helping us take a fresh look at an old book. Olesburg can help preachers "manuscript" the text, as mentioned in chapter one.

Peterson, Eugene. *Eat This Book: A Conversation in the Art of Spiritual Reading*. Grand Rapids: Eerdmans, 2006.

Peterson warmly invites us into *lectio divina*, the "holy reading" talked about in chapter one. His last chapter also describes his process of translating Scripture into the volume known as *The Message*.

Wilhoit, James C., and Evan B. Howard. *Discovering Lectio Divina: Bringing Scripture into Ordinary Life*. Downers Grove, IL: InterVarsity Press, 2012.

A practical, readable guide for inviting the Holy Spirit to use Scripture to shape our lives. Enjoyable and accessible for new believers, and novel and winsome enough for long-time believers to learn something new.

WEBSITES ABOUT PREACHING

If you preach the Revised Common Lectionary (or would like to try!), these are great places to start. And since many passages are included in the lectionary, even if you aren't a "lectionary preacher" you'll find good resources on many texts.

The Revised Common Lectionary, lectionary.library.vanderbilt.edu
> An introduction to the lectionary from the Vanderbilt Divinity Library, including a list of all passages, daily readings, frequently asked questions about the lectionary, and art and music for each Sunday.

The Text This Week, www.textweek.com
> A treasure-trove of resources on each text—illustrations, movies, art, biblical background and many links to other helpful sites.

Working Preacher, www.workingpreacher.org
> Preachers and professors offer commentary and sermon ideas for each of the four passages for every Sunday. You could print out the commentary for each week and use it in a small group.

If you want to listen to or watch other preachers:

Preaching Today, www.preachingtoday.com
> A great way to improve as a preacher is to watch and listen to other preachers. This site has hundreds of sermons available. Ask questions as you watch about the use of Scripture, grace, God language, delivery, images and so forth. A subscription is required to fully access all of the resources on the site. From the editors of *Leadership Journal.*

The Center for Excellence in Preaching, cep.calvinseminary.edu
> Hundreds of sermon starters, advice on which commentaries to choose, ideas for shaping the preaching calendar, plus many recordings (audio and video) of great preachers.

CONFERENCES YOU MAY WANT TO ATTEND

Q Ideas Conference
> If you enjoy new ideas, good speakers and thought-provoking

conversations—which may indirectly inspire your preaching—check out Q. There is a national conference each year, as well as regional events.

Calvin Symposium on Worship and the Arts

Three days of worship services, seminars and workshops on everything from preaching to worship planning. You'll hear at least five different preachers over the span of the conference.

The Festival of Homiletics

An annual event drawing preachers from across North America for a week of worship, workshops, small groups and lectures. Presenters and attendees tend to be from mainline American denominations.

Seminary Options

Many seminaries and larger churches offer preaching conferences, seminars and week-long classes. Check your region for options and look up these preaching institutes: Lloyd John Ogilvie Institute of Preaching at Fuller Theological Seminary, the Center for Preaching at Gordon-Conwell Theological Seminary, Engle Institute of Preaching at Princeton Theological Seminary, E. K. Bailey Preaching Conference at Southern Baptist Theological Seminary, and the Center for Excellence in Preaching at Calvin Theological Seminary.

Notes

Chapter 1: Biblical Preaching

[1]William Willimon, *Calling and Character: Virtues of the Ordained Life* (Nashville: Abingdon, 2000), 13-14.

[2]Eugene Peterson, *Eat This Book* (Grand Rapids: Eerdmans, 2006), xi.

[3]Ibid., 30-31.

[4]Barbara Brown Taylor, *The Preaching Life* (Lanham, MD: Rowman & Littlefield, 1993), 52.

[5]Lori Carrell, *The Great American Sermon Survey* (Wheaton, IL: Mainstay Church Resources, 2000), 108.

[6]Eugene Peterson, *Under the Unpredictable Plant* (Grand Rapids: Eerdmans, 1994), 39.

[7]Ibid., 95.

[8]Randy Bytwerk, speaking at the Preacher's Oasis, Calvin Theological Seminary, July 11, 2006.

[9]Tim Brown, homiletics class, Western Theological Seminary.

[10]The list of questions alone is worth the price of Wilson's book! When I get stuck in my writing, Wilson's questions help me move toward clarity. Read the entire list in Paul Scott Wilson, *The Practice of Preaching* (Nashville: Abingdon, 2007), 18-25.

[11]Taylor, *Preaching Life*, 80-82.

[12]Sidney Greidanus, *The Modern Preacher and the Ancient Text* (Grand Rapids: Eerdmans, 1988), 5.

CHAPTER 2: GOD-CENTERED PREACHING

[1]My thanks to Scott Hoezee for assistance with bird names. He also recommends an online search for the call of the Swainson's thrush, which is beautiful.

[2]Christian Smith and Melinda Lundquist Denton, *Soul Searching: The Religious and Spiritual Lives of American Teenagers* (New York: Oxford University Press, 2009).

[3]Ibid., 162-63.

[4]Westminster Confession of Faith, chap. 2, sect. 1, in *Creeds of the Churches*, ed. John Leith, 3rd ed. (Atlanta: John Knox Press, 1982), 197.

[5]Christian Smith, "On 'Moralistic Therapeutic Deism' as U.S. Teenagers' Actual, Tacit, De Facto Religious Faith," in *Religion and Youth*, ed. Sylvia Collins-Mayo and Pink Dandelion (Aldershot, UK: Ashgate, 2010), 41-46.

[6]Elizabeth Corrie, quoted in John Blake, "Author: More Teens Becoming 'Fake' Christians," CNN.com, August 27, 2010, www.cnn.com/2010/ LIVING /08/27/almost.christian.

[7]Dorothy Sayers, *Letters to a Diminished Church: Passionate Arguments for the Relevance of Christian Doctrine* (Nashville: Thomas Nelson, 2004), 114-15.

[8]Scott Hoezee, personal email, December 5, 2014.

[9]*Psalter Hymnal: Belgic Confession*, art. 1 (Grand Rapids: CRC Publications, 1987), 817.

[10]The Westminster Confession of Faith, chap. 2, sect. 1, in *The Book of Confessions*, www.pcusa.org/site_media/media/uploads/oga/pdf/boc2014.pdf.

[11]John Mark McMillan, "How He Loves," 2005.

[12]Lenny LeBlanc and Paul Baloche, "Above All," 1999.

[13]*Belgic Confession*, art. 8.

[14]Ibid.

[15]Ibid.

[16]Ibid., art. 22.

CHAPTER 3: GRACE-FULL PREACHING

[1]Philip Yancey, "Grace," *Philip Yancey.com*, accessed August 24, 2015, www .philipyancey.com/q-and-a-topics/grace. For more on this read Yancey's book *What's So Amazing About Grace?* (Grand Rapids: Zondervan, 1997).

[2]Horatio G. Spafford, "When Peace Like a River," 1873.

[3]Cornelius Plantinga Jr., *Not the Way It's Supposed to Be: A Breviary of Sin* (Grand Rapids: Eerdmans, 1995), 199.

[4]Paul Scott Wilson, *The Four Pages of a Sermon* (Nashville: Abingdon, 1999), 205-6.

[5]Ibid., 206.

[6]Carrie Steenwyk and John Witvliet, *The Worship Sourcebook*, 2nd ed. (Grand Rapids: Faith Alive, 2013), 348.

[7]Yancey, *What's So Amazing About Grace?* 45.

Chapter 4: Compelling Preaching

[1]Harry Emerson Fosdick, *The Living of These Days: The Autobiography of Harry Emerson Fosdick* (New York: Harper, 1956), 92.

[2]Haddon Robinson, *Biblical Preaching* (Grand Rapids: Baker, 1980), 32-33.

[3]I am indebted to Paul Scott Wilson. The structure here is the "Four Pages" model taught by him and described in his books *The Four Pages of the Sermon* (Nashville: Abingdon, 1999), and *The Practice of Preaching*, rev. ed. (Nashville: Abingdon, 2007). If you are seeking more clarity in your sermons, read Wilson.

[4]"*Baca*, an unknown desolate valley, becomes verdant as the pilgrims pass through" (*Cambridge Annotated Study Bible NRSV* [Cambridge: Cambridge University Press, 1993], 505). "The valley of Baca, i.e., 'the valley of weeping,' a normally dry valley where many balsam trees grew" (*NRSV Harper Study Bible* [Grand Rapids: Zondervan, 1991], 835).

[5]Wilson, *Four Pages of the Sermon*, 13, 16.

[6]Arthur Quiller-Couch, quoted in Forrest Wickman, "Who Really Said You Should 'Kill Your Darlings'?" *Slate.com*, October 18, 2013, www.slate.com /blogs/browbeat/2013/10/18/_kill_your_darlings_writing_advice_what _writer_really_said_to_murder_your.html.

[7]My thanks to Michael Le Roy, who spoke on the connection between an awake soul and leadership and gave me permission to use his ideas as a launching pad for this section.

Chapter 5: Imaginative Preaching

[1]For more on this, I recommend Scott Hoezee's book *Actuality: Real Life Stories for Sermons That Matter*, Artistry of Preaching Series (Nashville: Abingdon, 2014).

[2]Dan Amira, "15 Things You Might Not Know About the 'I Have a Dream' Speech," *New York Magazine*, August 28, 2013, www.nymag.com/daily /intelligencer/2013/08/i-have-a-dream-speech-facts-trivia.html.

[3]Tony Campolo, *It's Friday, But Sunday's Comin'* (Nashville: Thomas Nelson, 2002). Dr. Campolo is professor emeritus of sociology at Eastern University.

[4]Haddon Robinson, *Biblical Preaching* (Grand Rapids: Baker, 2001). This book was also discussed in chapter four.

[5]To learn more about using images in sermons, see Peter Jonker, *Preaching in Pictures: Using Images for Sermons That Connect*, Artistry of Preaching Series (Nashville: Abingdon, 2015).

CHAPTER 6: CONTEXTUAL PREACHING

[1]Joseph Parker, quoted in *Preach to Convince*, ed. James D. Berkley (Waco, TX: Word, 1986), 41.

[2]Scott Hoezee, personal email, December 5, 2014.

[3]"Sermon Evaluation Form," Calvin Theological Seminary, accessed August 25, 2015, http://cep.calvinseminary.edu/engageCongregation /sermonEvaluation/sermonEvaluationForm.pdf.

[4]Reuben Post Halleck, *History of English Literature*, 1900, quoted in Thomas Tapper and Percy Goetschius, *Essentials in Music History* (1923; repr., New York: Charles Scribner's, 2011), 42.

CHAPTER 7: RELEVANT PREACHING

[1]See George M. Stulac, *James*, IVP New Testament Commentary (Downers Grove, IL: IVP Academic, 1993); Ralph P. Martin, *James*, Word Biblical Commentary 48 (Nashville: Thomas Nelson, 1988); and Dan G. McCartney, *James*, Baker Exegetical Commentary on the New Testament (Grand Rapids: Baker Academic, 2009).

CHAPTER 8: EMBODIED PREACHING

[1]For more on this, see Robert Jacks, *Just Say the Word: Writing for the Ear* (Grand Rapids: Eerdmans, 1981).

[2]Robert Jacks, *Getting the Word Across: Speech Communication for Pastors and Lay Leaders* (Grand Rapids: Eerdmans, 1995).

CHAPTER 9: SELF-LESS PREACHING

[1]To learn more about this idea and to get ideas for books to read, I recommend Cornelius Plantinga Jr., *Reading for Preaching: The Preacher in Conversation with Storytellers, Biographers, Poets, and Journalists* (Grand Rapids: Eerdmans, 2013).

[2]Eugene Peterson, *Under the Unpredictable Plant* (Grand Rapids: Eerdmans, 1994), 49.

CHAPTER 10: GETTING FEEDBACK ABOUT YOUR PREACHING

[1]Frederick Buechner, *Telling Secrets* (San Francisco: Harper One, 1991), 61.

PRAXIS

EQUIPPING LEADERS FOR MINISTRY

"...TO EQUIP HIS PEOPLE FOR WORKS OF SERVICE,

SO THAT THE BODY OF CHRIST MAY BE BUILT UP."

EPHESIANS 4:12

God has called us to ministry. But it's not enough to have a vision for ministry if you don't have the practical skills for it. Nor is it enough to do the work of ministry if what you do is headed in the wrong direction. We need both vision *and* expertise for effective ministry. We need *praxis*.

Praxis puts theory into practice. It brings cutting-edge ministry expertise from visionary practitioners. You'll find sound biblical and theological foundations for ministry in the real world, with concrete examples for effective action and pastoral ministry. Praxis books are more than the "how to"—they're also the "why to." And because *being* is every bit as important as *doing*, Praxis attends to the inner life of the leader as well as the outer work of ministry. Feed your soul, and feed your ministry.

If you are called to ministry, you know you can't do it on your own. Let Praxis provide the companions you need to equip God's people for life in the kingdom.

www.ivpress.com/praxis

Finding the Textbook You Need

The IVP Academic Textbook Selector
is an online tool for instantly finding the IVP books
suitable for over 250 courses across 24 disciplines.

www.ivpress.com/academic/